THINKING
for a LIVING

CREATING IDEAS THAT REVITALIZE YOUR BUSINESS, CAREER & LIFE

JOEY REIMAN

LONGSTREET PRESS

Published by
LONGSTREET PPRESS, INC.
325 Milledge Avenue
Athens, Georgia 30601

Printed in the United States of America

Library of Congress Catalog Number 97-76265

ISBN: 1-56352-469-4

Jacket design by Elizabeth O'Dowd
Book design by Jill Dible

This book is about thinking. Therefore, it's dedicated to the ones I think most about: My wife, Cynthia, and my two sons, Alden and Julien.

TABLE OF CONTENTS

Thinking is the hardest work there is,
which is probably why so few engage in it.

— HENRY FORD

CHAPTER 1

How the Most Money I Never Made Taught Me How to Think for a Living

"An invasion of armies can be resisted,
but not an invasion of ideas."
— VICTOR HUGO

ON A FRIGID February day in Minneapolis in 1994, I did the unthinkable.

As my board of directors looked on with expressions ranging from disbelief, to horror, to apparent dread that my cheese had finally slipped off my cracker, I announced that I was going to shut down my advertising agency and open an ideas company. I told them I was going to think for a living.

This was a revolutionary and life-changing moment for someone who had been in advertising for twenty years and had gone from ad-world whiz kid to the head of a company with $100 million in sales. In effect, I was telling the powerful corporate honchos — sitting in stunned silence around a table that looked as if it had been built by the designers of Darth Vader's Imperial Warship — that their whole model for thinking about advertising, a business built on the primacy of ideas, was wrong, and that I had come up with a better one.

As each day goes by, I become more and more convinced that it wasn't just a revolutionary, life-changing moment for me. I got out of advertising because I was convinced it no longer mattered; that ad firms were producing so much clutter they couldn't effectively convey any ideas. But that's exactly what most of us face in whatever we do. We're drowning in information but desperate for direction, overloaded with data but unable to figure out what it means, bombarded with images and messages that tell us nothing, stuck in corporate structures in which numbers and facts endlessly multiply but good ideas never see the light of day.

WHAT'S THE BIG IDEA?

Now more than ever before what we need as businesses, as individuals, as a society is one thing: IDEAS. New, vital, raw, hot, bracing, challenging, paradigm-shattering ideas. Ideas that will keep you ahead of a business environment that changes as fast as the new technologies, which now compress what used to be decades of change into days. Ideas that will help keep families together and children whole and sane, in a world where most of the old expectations about families have long since gone out the window. That's what this book is about — the centrality of creative ideas in modern life and how to nurture and foster and create ones that will revitalize your business, your family, your being, and in the most profound way, our whole society. In fact, in order for all of us to prosper, perhaps even to survive, in the coming new century, we need to start thinking smarter, more comprehensively, more creatively. This book is a road map for how to do that.

I admit, it's a fairly tall order. But anyone who knows me or my work knows at least two things about me: (1) I'm a pretty good idea person, and everything I've ever done — from flying a mariachi band from Atlanta to Dallas to sing my praises to a big Mexican-food account I was pitching the next day (I got the job) to staging a fake white-collar drug bust, including cops with machine guns, as a way to lure my television-reporter girlfriend to the perfect place for me to propose marriage (I got the girl) — has come from no known mold, and (2) I've always thought big and figured the only limits are the ones we put on ourselves. That's why one of the ideas I'm proudest of is the campaign we did for the 1996 Paralympic movement, based on the incredible courage and fortitude of athletes who had overcome cerebral palsy or the loss of their legs to become phenomenal athletes. It's theme? "There are no hopeless bodies, only hopeless hearts." It asked the question to the rest of the world, "What's your excuse?"

So if there's something audacious in the notion that I can make a career out of thinking for a living or give others ideas on how to do it, it's no more audacious than anything else I've done in my life. This notion comes from some-one, after all, whose first undertaking after grad-uating from college was writing a movie script about two Jewish terrorists who kidnapped three hundred international debutantes and held them hostage until there was peace in the Middle East. I sent it off to the great film director Federico Fellini, who didn't make it into a movie but nonetheless invited me to study under him. It didn't make me a dime, but going to Rome for Fellini taught me something far more important. I learned about the magic of inspiration, the way a person's ideas, vision, and creativity can change lives in the way a pebble thrown into a pond sends out ripples far from the place it orig-inally lands.

That's another thing I hope this book will do — create lots of creative ripples, waves, and tides. If I have a passion in life, and perhaps a gift, it's a passion for ideas — big, small, pro-found, goofy, important, trivial. Ever since I was a kid, I've known that there was a straight, gray line that led to very predictable places and a spangled, zig-zag, make-it-up-as-you-go-along path, full of wild leaps and inspired non sequiturs, that was a heck of a lot more fun. That's the path I wanted to follow. And that's pretty much what I've done.

I HAD A GREAT TIME IN ADVERTISING

I never planned on going into advertising. I grew up on the Upper West side of Manhattan.

My mother was an astrologer, and my father was a food broker, and like so many other proud parents, they figured I might as well become President. I was more drawn to acting and became so obsessed with James Bond films that I persuaded my parents to send me to a school called St. Sergius so I could learn Russian, all the better to fight the Cold War. After college at Brandeis and my journey to study under Fellini, I came home and wrote a musical called, *Discovery — The True Story of Christopher Columbus*. This looked promising until the producer ran out of money before the play was staged.

I wasn't the most practical person in the world, but it was becoming clear even to me that offbeat musicals were not a sure-fire road to commercial success. In need of work, and under orders from my parents to find some, I wandered into what was then the Norman, Craig & Kummel advertising firm. My background in advertising at that point was limited to a bit performance as a young chef in a television ad for Eastern Airlines and I got the notion from watching Darrin Stephens on *Bewitched* that it might be a fun profession. Plus, I was very impressed with how fancy the offices were and how beautiful the people looked. I figured I might as well give it a shot. I leapfrogged from agency to agency for a few years, formed my own firm in 1986, and stayed on to build it up to a $100 million business.

I had a great time in advertising. My best idea was probably my first one as an entrepreneur — I decided to finance my company on a Visa card, and one thousand days later I sold that idea for $5 million. Along the way, I created some terrific ads based on some other pretty good ideas. My General Tire campaign introduced a new puncture-resistant tire. While the camera travels through New York City streets, scanning a hooker, a hubcap thief, a squeegee-wielder, potholes, broken bottles, and a fruit-filled wooden crate in the middle of the street, the city's former mayor Ed Koch advises, "Make sure you take new General puncture-resistant tires on your next trip to New York."

I also spearheaded the initial marketing effort to bring the 1996 Olympic Games to Atlanta by blanketing the city with outdoor boards targeted directly at members of the International Olympic Committee who were visiting town. And for Young and Tender Chicken, I created the first TV commercial ever to show eleven-month-old babies dancing the funky chicken. The TV spot got worldwide attention, winning an award at the Cannes Film Festival. But after a while it hit me that I didn't really want to create ads, I wanted to create *ideas*. But that isn't the way the advertising business works. I had

---

THE SHORTEST DISTANCE BETWEEN TWO IDEAS

IN 300 B.C., THE IDEA THAT EVERYTHING COULD BE DEDUCED FROM A FEW BASIC PRINCIPLES WAS A NEW AND IMPORTANT THOUGHT. THIS IDEA WAS CREATED BY A TEACHER IN ALEXANDRIA, EGYPT, NAMED EUCLID. HE ALSO THOUGHT UP THE IDEA OF GEOMETRY, LEADING THE WAY FOR OTHER THINKERS TO CREATE SOME PRETTY BIG IDEAS, TOO. ADDITONAL KUDOS GO TO GALILEO, COPERNICUS, AND NEWTON, STUDENTS OF EUCLID'S TEACHINGS.

built two well-known, national advertising agencies legendary for their superior creative work. Notice I use the words *creative work*, not *ideas*. Advertising agencies, since their inception, have been paid for executing ideas, not creating them. I use the word executing as in the "put-to-death" definition, because very often the execution itself buries the ideas, leaving us with mediocre advertisements. Hence, **the world is ad rich and idea poor.**

And this phenomenon is not limited to advertising.

A GOOD HAIR DAY FOR IDEAS

I once heard a story about a famous celebrity hairdresser who got a frantic call from a woman needing her hair styled immediately for an important gala that evening. The hairdresser rushed to the woman's home, asked for a ribbon, and proceeded to create his masterpiece using only a brush and the ribbon. Thirty minutes later her hair was done, and she was dazzled beyond belief.

"How much do I owe you?" she asked.

"$2,000," he replied.

She was stunned. "That's outrageous," she said. "I'm not going to pay $2,000 for a ribbon."

He looked at her cooly, gave the ribbon a quick tug, and watched his masterpiece instantly unravel into a shaggy mop of unruly curls and locks.

"That's fine," he said. "The ribbon is free."

Today American enterprise is primarily based on the value of ribbons; not just the hairdresser's ribbon, but all things we can touch — tangibles like bricks and mortar and fancy buildings and thirty-second spots. That's about to change. Today currency is the idea, but tomorrow ideas will be the currency. The insanely competitive, invent-it-today, reinvent-it-tomorrow world of business can no longer rely solely on capital, raw materials, and technology. Everyone has that stuff. It must now mine for the greatest gem of all — the idea.

THE MOST MONEY
I NEVER MADE

Advertising agencies get jobs by pitching ideas — in effect, giving them away for free. Once they get the account, they make their money by volume production. The more space bought, the more spots aired, the more print ads sold, the bigger the profit to the agency. Whatever creativity exists is free. Ad agencies don't charge where they add value — by coming up with great ideas. They charge where they add no value — the execution of ideas.

This revelation hit me a few years back while pitching the $10 million Days Inn Hotel account for the third time. Every time Days Inn appointed a new CEO, they would fire their advertising agency (mine) and we would have to repitch. My agency was up against New York's biggest and best agencies. I was told by the client that since Days' corporate offices were moving from Atlanta to New York, I should play it safe and not waste my time or money on an account I was not going to get.

The Safe Way is a grocery store, not a way to

run a business or live your life, so I figured if I could come up with a good enough idea, I could still get the job. In fact, I didn't come up with one, but my wife, Cynthia, did, and after presenting my idea in New York I got a phone call from the president of the company. He wanted to fly to Atlanta to talk with me. "Fabulous," I thought to myself. "I got the account."

When the chief executive landed at Hartsfield, he told me something different. He said he wanted to give the account to another firm, but he wanted to pay me for my big idea. A lot.

I went home and thought about it. I could take the money, having made more on one great idea than I'd ever made before. What I would lose, though, would be the ability to tell the press that I'd won the account three times in a row, the honor of having a huge company like Days Inns on my roster, and a good stroking for my big, fat ego. I called the CEO of Days Inn and said if he wanted my big idea, he had to give me the whole account. He did. The press rewarded me with big headlines, and my ego was rewarded the way gluttons reward themselves with hot fudge sundaes.

And then a peculiar thing happened. One year later, at our fourth-quarter finance meeting, I asked my CFO how much profit we'd made on the Days Inn account. He said rather than making money, we were heavily in the red because the account was so labor intensive we were spending more than we were taking in. Your ego can cloud your vision, but this time the message — the magnificent *Aha!* — was hard to miss. What had started out as a million-dollar idea lost all its financial worth because we were too busy managing the client instead of creating ideas.

It was a straight line from that *Aha!* to the meeting where I told my board I was releasing all my clients, cutting my staff from 150 to seventeen, and transforming my company from an ad agency to the world's first ideation firm that I called BrightHouse, which opened its doors June 27, 1995. It was based on the idea that one brilliant idea is more valuable than a million executions. Instead of coming up with commercials and jingles, some of America's biggest corporations pay us between $450,000 and $1 million to spend a month coming up with concepts and experiences based around the company's business. So far, it's worked better than I could have dreamed.

For Coty Perfumes we came up with the idea of Ghost Myst, the first perfume created to express a women's inner, rather than outer, beauty. It started a new-age fragrance movement and became a best-selling perfume in its first year, winning this country's most prestigious fragrance award — the Fifi.

If you went to the 1996 Summer Olympics, you probably made it to the Coca-Cola Olympic City, which took Coke and turned it into an experience for the mind, body, and spirit. By creating a multisensory environment, we allowed visitors to feel like real Olympians. In fact, the entrance to the event was an inverted stadium stand filled with cheering fans. Once inside, the experience continued as visitors participated in Olympic events. If you've been to Altanta's new

Turner Field, home of the Atlanta Braves, you need to experience Coca-Cola's Sky Field, for which we provided much of the thinking. Atlanta Braves management offered The Coca-Cola Company a jumbo scoreboard to advertise, but a billboard is not a meaningful experience. Instead we helped create a place for friends and family to gather and watch a baseball game. What was just an empty roof became a fun experience that enhances the game as well as creates an in-stadium presence for Coca-Cola. Steve Koonin of Coca-Cola says, "Five years ago we were just there. We were a concession product with advertising. Now we're a friend of the fan, and we're fun. And we're winning."

For Randstad Worldwide, which has approximately 200,000 E.W.'s (employees working), we created FlexLife, the idea that one of the most creative ways to work and live is to go from job to job and experience to experience.

Someday at the airport, you're likely to see Plane Delicious™, a gourmet meal in a shopping bag to replace the nightmare food (or, more often these days, the nonexistent food) on airplanes.

Someday at your pharmacy, you're likely to see my answer to the first-aid kit, the First Herb Kit™, with such herb-based remedies as aloe vera, echinacea, and ginger. You also might paint your house with Aroma Paint™, the first aroma-scented paint.

I'm not saying that every idea I've come up with is a great one. Don't ask me about my "Teller I Love You" promotion for a bank or Postman-Flavored Dog Food. Many of my colleagues also remember the time I created an antismoking billboard campaign. It showed a picture of a cemetery, and across the board it read, "SMOKING SECTION" in big type. Everyone thought it was a great idea except my largest client — RJR/Nabisco.

But I do know that one unassailably great idea I've had is the notion of thinking for a living, of betting all my chips on the idea that these days ideas are what matters most in business, in life, and in society.

It has been said that the definition of insanity is asking the same question over and over again and expecting a different answer. This book is about asking a lot of new questions. What kind of nutty idea is this? Not as nutty as you think. What's the value of an idea? Whatever you think it is. How can you think for a living? The same way you can start a company on a Visa card and build it up to a $5 million business — by worshipping at the altar of smart, innovative ideas, rewarding creativity, and knowing that every problem can breed a solution, and every solution can breed an even better one.

WELCOME TO THE IDEA CAPITAL OF AMERICA

There are two good reasons why my nutty idea about thinking for a living isn't so nutty. The first is where I live. Outsiders often think about Atlanta in terms of Rhett and Scarlet and Tara and the mythology of the Old South, but what's really made Atlanta such a phenomenal success is one thing — ideas. In fact, no other city can lay claim to more big ideas than Atlanta.

A pharmacist conjures up a soft drink around the idea of bringing people together, and it becomes the world's favorite soft drink and the best-known brand on the planet. A young black man living in the midst of segregation dreams an amazing dream, and his legacy inspires us to this day. A billboard salesman with a completely crazy idea about an all-news cable TV station comes up with the world's most far-reaching TV news network. Two men fired from their jobs create the largest do-it-yourself retail concept in the world. A real estate broker and former football player with the preposterous idea of bringing the Olympics to Atlanta somehow pulls it off. A woman with a passion for Civil War history and a romantic notion about the antebellum South writes a book that becomes the world's best-seller next to the Bible and the ultimate experience in American film. General Sherman may have burned Atlanta to the ground in the Civil War, but the ideas created here now light up the world, which is precisely why corporate America loves Atlanta and why the population of the city has grown so much.

The second reason my idea isn't so nutty is

WINNING IDEA

HE CREATED THE CENTER SNAP IN 1893. HE CONCEIVED OF DIVIDING A FOOTBALL GAME INTO FOUR QUARTERS. HE ALSO CREATED THE ATHLETIC DORMITORY. HE PICKED UP DOZENS OF TROPHIES FOR ALL HIS IDEAS, AND NOW FOOTBALL'S FINEST COMPETE FOR HIS TROPHY. MEET JOHN HEISMAN.

where we all reside. We are living at the most creative moment in world history, where the end of Communism, the growth of global markets, and astounding revolutions in technology have made this the Golden Age of ideas. For most of the world's history, great ideas didn't mean great reality. There was too much to get in the way. The pace of technological change was too slow, the government was too oppressive, the country was too poor, the corporation was too hidebound. It took more than a great idea to make a great change. Now, for the first time in history, none of that is true for millions upon millions of people; barriers fall around the world every day.

Ideas are now the currency. This means two very big things. The first is what it means for you. It means if you think smart, live creatively, and make sure you capitalize on your ideas, your potential is limitless. The second is what it means for all of us together. We live at a time when creative people can transform cultures in ways that used to be unimaginable. Do it right, and you don't just push yourself to a new level, you have the potential to move all of us along as well.

CHAPTER 2

THE GOLDEN AGE OF IDEAS AND NINE THINKERS WHO FIGURED OUT HOW TO MAKE IT WORK FOR THEM

One day, mother of future Microsoft mogul Bill Gates walked in on her young son to find him sitting there doing nothing. She asked Bill what he was doing. "I'm thinking, Mom, I'm thinking."

OPEN AN ISSUE of *Town & Country* magazine in the year 2005. The feature story describes the new millenium's ultimate gift: an idea. Touted as the new luxury, an idea can now be bought for the love of your life, for your childen, for your best friend. Ideas range from "Pairfume"™ — a perfume that activates when two bodies touch — to the first Moving Theater — a three-dimensional experiential movie theater that literally puts you in the picture. Then there is a little gift for your spouse, who is a gynecologist and owns a boat — a name for the boat, "Sea Section." All ideas come with your own copyright or patent in your name from the U.S. government. The prices for these ideas range from a thousand dollars to $10 million. Too pricey? Not if you consider that tomorrow's wealthy will be the people with the best and most ideas.

The *Town & Country* scenario is not unlikely, given what companies pay today for a good idea. BrightHouse charges up to $1 million for an idea. As a matter of fact, the average price for a consulting firm to deliver a strategic idea to a company is $750,000. Ideas are replacing the bricks and mortar of businesses around the world, and for good reason. You can't get to the 21st century on cruise control. You need ideas, the fuel of the future.

Now let's flip back to 1918 and pick up an issue of *Forbes* magazine. Here you'll find a list of the thirty wealthiest men in America. Not surprisingly, most of their fortunes came from turning raw materials into manufactured goods. It seems that if you had enough oil, chemicals, or metal, you could hang out with Rockefeller.

In fact, John D. Rockefeller proved that you could turn steel into gold. But consider how little he had to think about. Steel was melted down and sold. The bigger the melt, the bigger the mint. Perhaps Rockefeller's best idea was his revelation to build more factories, knowing full-well that volume was his ticket to financial acclaim. In contrast, as you can see from the list below, most of today's richest people owe their fortunes to raw thinking.

ONE HUNDRED WEALTHIEST AMERICANS, ACCORDING TO FORBES MAGAZINE MONDAY, SEPTEMBER 29, 1997

NAME	MAIN SOURCE OF INCOME	ESTIMATED NET WORTH IN BILLIONS
William H. Gates III	Microsoft	$ 39.80 billion
Warren Edward Buffett	investor	$ 21.00
Paul Gardner Allen	Microsoft	$ 17.00
Lawrence Joseph Ellison	Oracle Corp. software	$ 9.20
Gordon Earl Moore	Intel Corp. computer chips	$ 8.80
Steven Anthony Ballmer	Microsoft	$ 8.30
John Werner Kluge	investments	$ 7.80
Ronald Owen Perelman	investments	$ 6.50
Jim C. Walton	Wal-Mart	$ 6.50
Helen R. Walton	Wal-Mart	$ 6.40
Alice L. Walton	Wal-Mart	$ 6.30
John T. Walton	Wal-Mart	$ 6.30
S. Robson Walton	Wal-Mart	$ 6.30
Jay Arthur Pritzker	finance & hotels	$ 6.00
Robert Alan Pritzker	manufacturer	$ 6.00
Michael Austin Dell	Dell Computer	$ 5.50
Philip H. Knight	Nike athletic apparel	$ 5.40
Philip F. Anschutz	oil & railroads	$ 5.20
Barbara Cox Anthony	media	$ 5.00
Anne Cox Chambers	media	$ 5.00

The media industry has elevated Anne Cox Chambers, John Kluge, and Ron Perelman to the nation's "twenty wealthiest," and Rupert Murdoch, Sumner Redstone, and Ted Turner made the list last year. All six own enterprises with material assets — motion pictures, studios, TV stations, video stores, and newspapers and publishing houses. Yet it is not in these assets that the money was made, but in the ideas and images that these men and women created.

THE IDEA AGE

Gone is the Industrial Age. That was a time when wealth was measured by volume and weight. Take the railroad freight service, for example. In 1860, 55 million tons of goods traveled by mail; in 1870, 72.5 million, and in 1885, 437 million tons. Today the industries of the mind ship tons of idea freight that travel in nanoseconds. Furthermore, the weight of an idea is no longer measured by a scale. Steel weighs far more than microchips, but microchips are far more valuable than steel.

Companies also weigh less than they used to. Have you ever been to a steel mill and seen three thousand men pouring tons of hot metal into big steel cauldrons? Contrast that scene with Netscape Communications, a multibillion dollar company that did not exist three years ago and has fewer than twenty-five full-time staffers. Nokia is a Finnish electronics company that has annual sales near $160 million and only five employees.

Ideas don't take up a lot of space. When Bill Gates built Microsoft, he constructed it out of thin air. His intellectual success did not compute with IBM. After all, IBM sold things like big mainframes. Microsoft never owned a factory.

Little did IBM know that Microsoft was not only a threat to IBM's antiquated, hard-driving company, but that Microsoft was just a micro-cosm of what was to come.

Phil Knight, CEO of Nike, did not make his fortune by selling a sneaker that could help your feet run faster, but by running a company that could think faster on its feet. Nike doesn't make shoes. They produce ideas that just do it for us. Bravery, women's rights, empowerment, and the pursuit of happiness are ideas that people will jump through hoops for. Ask someone from Nike what business they're in, and they will respond, "The business of life."

Ideas that inspire companies affect not only the corporate pocket but the corporate heart. Many companies today have integrated "cause marketing" efforts into their corporate culture. Anita Rodderick's Body Shop had the idea to ban animal testing when creating new cosmetics. She turned her philosophical idea into an eco-nomic windfall.

Akio Morita, cofounder of Sony, likes to tell a story that reveals his company's philosophy of creating ideas. Two shoe salesmen find them-selves in a backward part of Africa. The first salesman sends a telegram back to the office: "There are no potential customers here. The natives don't wear shoes." The other salesman wires: "No one wears shoes here. We can domi-nate the market. Send all possible stock." The pocket radio, digital camera, and Sony Walkman are all results of ideas based on Morita's motto, "When there is no market, create one."

We know that the most creative corporations

are also the most profitable. Such companies as Microsoft and Sony have taught us that creativity is the engine of profitability — a necessary condition, not a contradiction. They have taught us that ideas are more important and more valuable than hardware, infrastructure, and delivery systems. These are examples of an idea whose time has come . . . **the idea.**

IDEAS BUILD COMPANIES

Twenty years ago when the GGT Group (a worldwide advertising network) was formed, it was a widely held view that small, creative ad shops, perhaps like great artists, could never be financially successful. Financial success was considered the preserve of the large, the boring, and the bureaucratic.

Today we know better. We know that the roads to success have many toll booths, that they don't all look the same, and that the ones built on the best ideas are the ones best able to get you where you want to go.

And so it is with GGT. As Michael Greenlees, CEO of an advertising empire, says, "Ideas is the business that we are in. It is the size and value of our ideas that set us apart from our competition."

GSD&M is one of America's biggest and best advertising agencies. Being located in Austin, Texas, hasn't stopped the likes of Wal-Mart, Fannie Mae, or Mastercard from knocking on GSD&M's door and handing over their businesses.

The company's chief executive, Roy Spence, believes as I do that ideas must be sold before ads. Not surprisingly, GSD&M has named its newly constructed building "Idea City."

Recently they won the newly formed Steel Alliance account. This prestigious $100 million account wanted the agency to find a way to get Americans to fall back in love with steel. The relationship between steel maker and steel buyer was at an all-time low. Thirty years ago the steel business lost the can to aluminum. Now the car business may be threatened. Years ago, cars were made of steel. Sit in the driver's seat today, and you're surrounded by a plastic dash and plastic cup holders, and all this plastic is surrounded by aluminum.

The agency knew that selling the *strength* of steel wouldn't have much muscle with a marketplace that wanted a metal that was lighter and cheaper. What they decided to sell was something invisible. They sold the idea of security. Steel is strong, therefore you're secure. Security is an idea, not a two-by-four. The result was a campaign touting the peace of mind we all get when we feel secure.

THE IDEA THAT LIT UP AMERICA

YOU WOULD NEED LOTS OF ENERGY TO CREATE AS MANY IDEAS AS BEN FRANKLIN DID. NO WONDER HE INVENTED THE BATTERY. KNOWN FOR HIS KITE FLYING, WHICH PROVED THAT ELECTRICITY AND LIGHTNING ARE ONE IN THE SAME, MR. FRANKLIN'S IDEA CAREER REALLY TOOK OFF WHEN HE HELPED DRAFT THE DECLARATION OF INDEPENDENCE AND THE U.S. CONSTITUTION. IN HIS SPARE TIME, HE CREATED A NEW TYPE OF BATHTUB, BIFOCAL GLASSES, AN IRONING MACHINE, AND HE WROTE POOR RICHARD'S ALMANAC, WHICH GAVE US THOUSANDS OF TRUISM'S SUCH AS "FISH & VISITORS SMELL AFTER THREE DAYS."

I'm told that advertising agencies all over the world are trying to jump on the bandwagon of selling ideas rather than ads. Saatchi & Saatchi dropped the word *advertising* to avoid being boxed in. But it takes more than repositioning to produce real change.

Intellectual Capital — The New Currency

Ideas used to be free. If you had a good one, you might tell someone about it or tinker with it. But unless they turned into something that produced a revenue stream, ideas were considered the folly of the avant-garde, ranging from eccentric professors to wild ad guys. Even when ideas saw the light of day, the active thinker rarely got the financial credit. The spoils would go instead to the financially adroit businessmen who profited from others' big ideas.

That's the old way of doing business. In the next century, the winners will be those with the best ideas. Small ideas will be worth a small sum, and big ideas will be priceless. Ideas that make money will cost money. The most valuable rewards will go to the ideas with the most value. The age of the big thinker has finally come — **an era where the profits will go to the prophets.**

Nine Characteristics of Big Thinkers

Big thinkers are the most valuable human beings on earth because they can unlock our imaginations. And what do big thinkers have in common? What makes them special? I've come up with nine characteristics of great thinkers:

1. Big thinkers are on fire.
2. Big thinkers never lose in their imaginations.
3. Big thinkers bet the farm.
4. Big thinkers marinate in thought.
5. Big thinkers think better together.
6. Big thinkers don't take no for an answer.
7. Big thinkers turn reality into fantasy.
8. Big thinkers live their lives with a purpose.
9. Big thinkers think with their hearts.

BIG THINKERS USE THE OTHER 90 PERCENT OF THEIR BRAINS

Today the most valuable piece of real estate measures less than one foot and is worth trillions, yet most of it remains uninhabited. This place is called your brain.

It has been hypothesized that most people use only 10 percent of their brains to think. That's too small a piece of our command center to be operational. Imagine living in a house or working in an office 10 percent of the size you're used to today.

Ten percent of any space is too little for big ideas. This is why we're always encouraged to "think outside the box." What we are really being told is to use the other 90 percent of our brains. Put another way, we are being encouraged to increase our percentage of creating something meaningful.

People who think outside the square run cir-

cles around people who don't. These big
thinkers inspire us, enlighten us, and change
the way we think forever. Here are nine very
different thinkers who have gotten me "out of
the box" and inspired me to explore the far
reaches of my mind. Like great athletes or
great artists, no two great thinkers are quite
alike. Some exemplify qualities that others on
my list don't. But as a group, they are a
remarkable advertisement for the qualities,
habits, and predilections that make great
thinkers and great successes.

TED TURNER

Ted Turner is on fire. I remember seeing him
at a cable TV conference in 1980. The people lis-
tening to his speech about the limitless future of
cable thought this man had escaped from a
loony bin. In fact, he had escaped from small
thinking. Turner is also the ultimate risk taker.
"I never quit. I've got a bunch of flags on my
boat. But there ain't no white flags. I don't sur-
render," says Captain Courageous.

Turner's thought actually bends risk into
reward. The great American psychologist and
educator William James gave an eloquent testi-
monial to the importance of risk taking in life
and business. "It is only by risking our persons
from one hour to another that we live at all. And
often enough, our fate beforehand, in an uncer-
tified result, is the only thing that makes the
result come true." As a man thinketh, so he is,
was the premise for my musical, *Discovery*.
Afraid of falling off the earth, the star of the

show sings, "First you think it, then you've done it . . . A man never knows until he tries."

Turner's ideas and his fire-breathing commitment to making them happen have changed the world forever. Futurist and author Alvin Toffler describes CNN as perhaps the most influential broadcast news source in the United States. Turner does not break the mold, he obliterates it. I worked for the Turner organization to help them launch the Cartoon Network, now one of the most successful enterprises on television. It was there that I learned big thinkers never lose in their imaginations. Ted Turner became a billionaire in 1990 because of an idea. The idea wasn't the amazing potential of cable, he said. It was the indomitable power of the human will. "Never get discouraged, and never quit," he said. "Because if you never quit, you're never beaten."

FEDERICO FELLINI

Big thinkers can turn their dreams into reality, but they can also do something more. They can create magic, turning reality into fantasy and fantasy into reality. Picasso did this. So did Jim Henson. So did Martha Graham and Miles Davis. But no one did it better than the great movie director Federico Fellini.

I met Fellini in 1975 at Cinicita Studios in Rome, Italy. The "Great Maestro," as he was known, welcomed me by offering me a seat across from his own. I felt as if I were speaking to the Creator. Perhaps I was, because Fellini has created many of the world's greatest films.

Fellini was an illustrator more than simply a director. He didn't *make* movies, he painted them. If Turner burns with a vision for building a company, Fellini burned with the incandescent power to create magic and then to re-create and reconfigure it over and over again. As a matter of fact, he often shot outdoor scenes inside the studio to make sure he had total control over his environment. In this way, he could take reality and recast it in his own image.

Fellini was not a big believer in screenplays but rather an artist who loved to play with the screen. Once an actress demanded a screenplay from him before accepting a part. Pressured to deliver a script, Fellini sent a two-hundred-page masterpiece to her. It was blank. Fellini emphatically believed that words were invented to move pictures. They would also move me.

My plan was to work for him as an apprentice on the motion picture *Casanova* starring Donald Sutherland, but, as you'll read later, my script had a very surprising turn. What I learned from Fellini was not about how to make a great movie, but how to live my life like it was a movie, how to be inspired by a vision of endless, regenerating creativity.

In a sense, Fellini was a control freak. In his Academy Award-winning film *Armarcord*, which means "I remember" in the dialect of the region he was born, Fellini recreates his boyhood in vivid detail. He was a man who saw people as paints and his memories as his environment. He lived in his own world and created such an alluring place that everyone in the world wanted to jet in.

Ten percent of Fellini's brain was built in the real world. The other 90 percent built a much better one.

FRED SMITH

Many of you know Fred Smith's story. He was the person who absolutely, positively had to be there. And he got there. His company should have died five or six times in the first three or four years, but by sheer courage and ferocious faith in his idea, he pulled off a miracle. Everyone told Fred Smith he was crazy to start an overnight package express service. But Smith, acting as a true visionary personality, listened to only one person — himself. And in 1983, Federal Express became the fastest company in history to achieve a billion dollars in revenue. All because "No" was not in his vocabulary.

Like other great thinkers, Fred Smith takes risks, he competes fiercely, and he leads with an indelible sense of personal commitment. His overnight delivery service operation has changed the way the world does business, but when he began almost no one thought he could succeed. He first outlined the idea for the company in a term paper he wrote at Yale. He got a C for his efforts. The professor gave Fred all the standard reasons why his idea was not valid — federal airline regulations, the capital required, the competition of large airlines, etc. But Smith was a man with an idea and a mission. He was undaunted by his professor's skepticism. He knew he could absolutely, positively pull it off. And, in the end, he did.

STEVEN JOBS

Steven Jobs is one of my favorite thinkers because he's the gentleman who defined what a big idea is. As he put it, a big idea is "an idea that makes a dent in the universe." Steve Jobs didn't actually invent the first Apple personal computer. That honor goes to Steve Wozniak. However, Steve Jobs was the nurturer of the idea. Without his energy and dedication to Apple, the computer would have taken a very different course. As Gene Landrum, author of *Profiles of Genius*, put it, "In a classical style and resolve of innovative geniuses, Jobs and Wozniak persevered in the face of imminent failure. Great innovators are successful because they are not aware of their limitations. They do not know what the experts know, so they go where the experts don't go, and are pleasantly shocked by what they learn."

Jobs and Wozniak did not have impressive technological credentials. They didn't even have the equivalent of a college education between them. But they did have a belief and a vision and a risk taking nature that created a market

---

A QUANTUM IDEA

WHEN HE WAS TWENTY-SIX, ALBERT EINSTEIN SUBMITTED THREE PAPERS TO THE GERMAN PERIODICAL "ANNALS OF PHYSICS" ENTITLED, *Special Theory of Relativity*, *The General Theory of Relativity*, AND *The Unified Field Theory*. ALL WERE ACCEPTED. WHAT'S MORE, A NEW BRANCH OF PHYSICS WAS CREATED — THE QUANTUM THEORY. EINSTEIN SAID, "IMAGINATION IS MORE IMPORTANT THAN KNOWLEDGE."

that would reach $30 billion in five years.

To get Apple off the ground, Jobs actually went out and begged for money for an unknown concept. The Jobs philosophy was "my way or the highway." Failure did not compute for Steven Jobs. Even when he was thrown out of his own organization, he started a new one. It was called Next. And now we find Steven Jobs back at Apple, recreating Apple as well as Pixar Animation Studios, which he says will keep pace with Disney: one major animated film a year. The movie *Toy Story* proves he's not kidding around. The 90 percent that Jobs used was his ability to reinvent, not just invent. This quality makes thinkers into winners before their competitors even appear on the screen, and then it makes them winners again while their competitors are trying to catch up to their first idea.

WALT DISNEY

His mission was to make the world smile. He would approach more than three hundred banks to get a loan for what many would have called a Mickey Mouse idea, but Walt Disney prevailed. The 302nd bank lent him money to build his dream. Disney stands alone in his ability to capture the imagination of both children and adults. Disney's secret was not to be found in the Mouseketeers, but in his *imagineers*. He coined the term *imagineering*, which still is the creative engine that puts the magic in the kingdom. Imagineers were and still are Disney.

Disney believed in feature animation when everybody else thought it was loony, and he con-

ceived and orchestrated some of the greatest animated features of all time. However, collaboration — bringing people together — was his
greatest achievement. Even Mickey Mouse, the
most purely Walt of any of his creations, was a
collaboration. It was Walt who decided, in
1928, that his new cartoon character would be a
mouse. And Walt actually provided the voice for
the mouse who would become Mickey in Walt's
first cartoon, "Steamboat Willie." But it was fellow cartoonist Ub Iwerks who did virtually all
the drawing, and even Walt's wife played a vital
role when she advised him to name the charismatic rodent Mickey instead of Mortimer.

As writer John Briggs observes, "Collaboration
is one of the best-kept secrets in creativity."
Actually, collaboration has been around for quite
some time. Thirteen people worked with
Michelangelo on the Sistine Chapel. The
Manhattan Project was a group, not a person,
that created the atomic bomb. Putting a man on
the moon was one of the most complicated collaborative efforts of all time. When Walt Disney
received a special Academy Award for *Snow
White and the Seven Dwarfs* in 1939, symbolized
by one big Oscar and seven little ones, he didn't
thank all 750 artists who worked on the picture.
I have no information as to what those artists
were paid, but I imagine that the profits, again,
did not go to the prophets.

Nonetheless, the group at Disney was able to
generate and develop many more ideas than any
individual could. "Never doubt that a small
group of thoughtful, committed people can
change the world. Indeed, it is the only thing

that ever has," Margaret Mead once wrote. And Disney's success as an individual and as a company is one of the most dramatic examples of a collaborative approach that allowed ideas to marinate and evolve and change until they reached their full potential. Rather than a blinding spark of inspiration, it has been collaboration and marination that has made Walt Disney's vision such an astoundingly successful one. And when it came to leadership, he kept his staff's level of aspiration high. He had one rule that stood above all others, and that was, whatever Disney did, it had to be better than what anybody else could do. To this day, that big, bold thought is at the heart of the Disney company's continuing success.

MARTIN LUTHER KING, JR.

I was at summer camp when Martin Luther King, Jr., gave his "I Have a Dream" speech in Washington, D.C. I watched it on TV, and ever since I've never forgotten the light in that man's eyes. He had been to the mountain, and I wanted to get there too.

King was a minister who became a prophet of peace and civil rights. He turned nonviolent protest into a holy crusade that eventually tore down the evil empire of white supremacy and segregtion in the South. I had never been to nor seen a sit-in, but his speech made me sit down and think. His words not only painted a future of racial harmony but put me in the picture. Sitting there at my summer camp, I realized there were no black kids in the bunks. The only black people I remember that summer were on that television screen. It took Martin Luther King's words and passion to make me think. His thoughts started a chain reaction that got the rest of us thinking as well.

One test of a great thinker is how far his thoughts travel. King's ideas marinated inside my head and inside the nation's soul for decades to come. Part of his genius is that his assassination couldn't kill his thoughts, it only made them seem richer, more powerful, more important. In the end, he taught us that racism is the absence of thinking. When you don't think, you become ignorant. Not thinking anywhere is a threat to thinking everywhere, but King's legacy is that a big, empowering legacy of courage, hope, and brotherhood can outlast the meanest and most hateful dullards and scoundrels. If that's not a big, important thought, I don't know what is.

King knew that dull thought was the enemy of a rich life. "Nothing pains some people more than having to think," he once said. He knew that thinking means being more tolerant of ideas and making an attempt to understand them. And he knew also that powerful ideas win out in the end, but it can take years, even decades, for that to happen. Native Americans were considered wise only when they became elders. Movements are like that, too. When the creed was written, "We hold these Truths to be self-evident, that all men are created equal . . ." it would take years of marination before people realized what a great idea that was. That summer while I was at camp, one man stood before the world and said, "I have a dream that one day this nation will rise up and live out the true meaning of this creed."

Martin Luther King's vision is proof that there is one thing stronger than all the hatred in the world, and that is an idea — a big thought — whose time has come.

SERGIO ZYMAN

If great thinkers live their lives with a purpose, is it any surprise that the most focused man I have ever met is behind the most recognized trademark on the planet?

Sergio Zyman is the former Senior Vice President and Chief Marketing Officer of The Coca-Cola Company, the world's largest beverage company and the leading producer and marketer of soft drinks. *Fortune* magazine named The Coca-Cola Company "America's Most Admired Company" for 1995 and 1996 in its annual "Corporate Reputations Survey." Two hundred countries enjoy the company's products at a rate of more than one billion servings a day. And if you ask insiders to name the person responsible for that, along with the late CEO Roberto Goizueta, Zyman's name is one of those most likely to bubble to the top.

A native of Mexico City, Zyman attended graduate schools in London, Paris, Jerusalem, and at Harvard University's Advanced Management and Corporate Financial Management programs, which must have taught him that failure is part of the journey to success. It's only when you stop at failure that you really fail.

He helped develop and introduce Diet Coke, a

great success, and New Coke, a famous flop. But like Babe Ruth, who broke the record for strike-outs, and Henry Ford, who went bankrupt, and Walt Disney, who was fired by an ad agency for not being able to draw, Zyman came out of New Coke as a new man. Like Friedrich Nietzche, who wrote, "Whatever doesn't kill me makes me stronger," Zyman turned his stumble into an unbeaten track record of victories.

Zyman has said many times that he doesn't need advertising agencies, he needs **ideas**. In Japan alone, he helped create thirty to forty new product brands in one year. And he's never forgotten that ideas come first. I asked Zyman, "Who deserves the financial reward for Coke's success — people like him who've built the company, or the pharmacist who invented the formula for Coke?" Without blinking he picked the pharmacist, paying homage to the big idea that started the company in the first place.

Zyman is also responsible for the philosophy, "Everything communicates." He knows that Coke has to reach consumers, not just through ads but through impressions, experiences, and unconventional avenues that touch the mind, body, and spirit, such as Coke's Olympic City at the 1996 Atlanta Olympics. Today Zyman directs a multibillion-dollar global marketing organization, one that never stops thinking, never stops looking for new ways to communicate. His dynamic "Always Coca-Cola" leadership has brought distinction to the Coke brand and has contributed significantly to his company's earnings of $3.5 billion in 1996. Ninety percent of Zyman's brain is filled with all focus and no fear. The late visionary and Coca-Cola CEO Roberto Goizueta once said, "Sergio is a producer of a change in our thinking."

TONY VOLPENTEST, YVONNE HOPF, AND FELLOW PARALYMPIANS

There's a wonderful story about the gods of Olympus who gather one day to answer a perplexing question: *Where should we hide the powers of the gods so the humans can't find them?*

One god says, "Let's hide them at the bottom of the sea."

"No," balks another. "They'll surely find them there. Let's put them at the top of the highest mountain, instead."

"No, no, no," answers the first. "They'll be up there before you know it."

After much discussion, the gods finally agree on where to hide their powers. They agree on a place they're certain that humans will never look — inside their own hearts.

Sorry, Olympic gods, but you haven't been to the Paralympic Games.

"To be surrounded by people who believe in you is one of life's precious gifts," the actor

---

FINEST IDEA

HE SAID, "THE EMPIRES OF THE FUTURE ARE THE EMPIRES OF THE MIND." NICKNAMED "THE BULLDOG" BY HIS GRANDMOTHER, MANY BELIEVE SIR WINSTON CHURCHILL WAS ENGLAND'S FINEST IDEA. AT THE VERY LEAST, NEVER HAS ONE IDEA DONE SO MUCH FOR SO MANY.

Christopher Reeve told a crowd of 64,588 at the Atlanta Paralympics in 1996. What was even more moving, I thought as I sat in the crowd, was that these seemingly impaired athletes had elevated their spirits to heights most of us could not even imagine. They had turned their thoughts into wings.

Tony Volpentest ran one hundred meters in 11.36 seconds on a pair of prosthetic feet. Visually impaired German swimmer Yvonne Hopf shaved two seconds off the world record in the women's one-hundred-meter freestyle event, finishing in just under one minute.

I had been given the assignment to market the event. What I learned was that these athletes were not disabled, they were *superabled*. The Olympics is where heroes are made. The Paralympics is where heroes come. These athletes teach us much about what the body can do. But they teach us much more about thinking, about what humans can do when they focus their minds and souls and entire beings on a task. The body has its own wisdom, and there are few things more revealing or more instructive than what happens when special athletes, with what most of us take to be daunting physical limitations, dream superhuman dreams and somehow make them come true.

MOTHER TERESA

I was on a plane when my beeper, which also sends out news bulletins, informed me that the most recognized and spiritual leader in the world, Mother Teresa, had died. Though I'm not

Catholic, I felt a great sense of loss. I imagine my grief was not because we had lost a religious leader but because Mother Teresa embodied perhaps the best part of thinking — our ability to transcend ourselves and turn thinking into healing.

Mother Teresa is associated more with good deeds than brilliant thoughts, but of course, good deeds, human compassion, and an intuitive sense of the needs of others represent the most profound thinking of all. And as one of the century's great healers, Mother Teresa was one of its greatest thinkers as well. Her life proves that faith is the gift. Religion is only the wrapping. And faith — true, abiding, empowering faith — is one of the biggest thoughts of all.

Her faith fueled her heart in a relentless effort to help the poor, the downtrodden, and the diseased. But her faith also taught us a lesson of enduring majesty. "Poverty doesn't only consist of being hungry for bread," she said, "but rather it is a tremendous hunger for human dignity. We need to love and to be somebody for someone else." That day on the plane, the word *humankind* took on a different meaning — that of a *human* who was indeed *kind*. It was only one of the many lessons this remarkable thinker conveyed.

MOTHERS OF INVENTION

Though Mother Teresa is the only woman on my impossibly short list of favorite thinkers, there are dozens of others who leap to mind. Oprah Winfrey is more than a talk-show host. She's someone who has changed the way we think. She has mixed passion with compassion in a way that's changed the vocabulary of television, taking what could be banal subjects from everyday life and turning them into the stuff of creative self-exploration.

Madonna's mixture of sensuality and theater changed the music industry; Roseanne's brash, earthy, in-your-face approach to issues of gender and class broke barriers on television; Donna Karan cut new patterns in fashion; Helen Gurley Brown made us all more cosmopolitan; Anita Roddick created an industry for every body; Katherine Graham created news; Barbara Walters made it entertaining; Ruth Bader Ginsburg and Sandra Day O'Connor surveyed our laws; and Madeleine Korbel Albright, Margaret Thatcher, and Hillary Rodham Clinton changed our minds about the heads of state and the role of women in politics. Heaven only knows the effect Princess Diana, even in death, eventually will have on modern society.

But all of these women exemplify the range of and potential for creative, break-the-mold thinking to produce economic, political, and social change.

The important thing to remember is how many paths there are to the light, how many qualities go into great thinking, how diverse great thinkers turn out to be. Ted Turner is not Mother Teresa, who is not Steven Jobs, who is not Walt Disney. But if we look at great thinkers, what we learn is amazingly clear. Thinkers who are dynamic and resourceful, who never give up, whose spirit is on fire, and who live with a purpose come in different fields with different visions. But they all can find ways to change the world. If we learn from them, we can too.

THE LIGHTBULB SOCIETY

The Hindus worshipped Devas, derived from the old Sanskrit *div*, meaning *brightness*. In other words, gods were their lightbulbs. Today we are a nation of lightbulbs — all of us feeling our way in the dark, trying to turn on some light or, if we are lucky enough, to "see the light."

In life we seek the proverbial "light at the end of the tunnel." In death, we believe we actually go to the light. When we have an idea we often say, "I've seen the light." The bottom line is that we are drawn to light as all living things are.

Perhaps it's an idea that helps a relationship at home or at work heal. Maybe it's an idea that improves our physical well being. Many of us are hoping that some light will shine on our problems, our bad habits, or our dysfunctional families. America's companies look for lightbulbs, too — illuminations that will light their stakeholders' imaginations. Bright ideas can put money in your pocket or add richness to your soul. God is an idea that has switched on more lightbulbs than all the power companies in the world.

A HEALING IDEA

EARLE AND JOSEPHINE DICKSON GOT HITCHED IN 1920 AND SETTLED DOWN IN NEW BRUNSWICK, NEW JERSEY. JOSEPHINE WAS ALWAYS CUTTING HER FINGERS IN THE KITCHEN. HER DOTING HUSBAND TENDED TO HER WOUNDS BY BALLING UP SOME GAUZE AND ATTACHING ADHESIVE TAPE. HIS THOUGHTFUL GIFT TO HER WOULD EVENTUALLY CATCH THE EYE OF MANAGEMENT AT JOHNSON & JOHNSON AND THE BAND-AID WAS BORN.

CHAPTER 3

BEWITCHED, BOTHERED, AND BEWILDERED: HOW ADVERTISING (AND THE REST OF US) LOST THE IDEAS GAME

"There's never a reason for a study if your idea is conceptually sound. You have to have confidence in your own ideas. I never did a market study on CNN. I do my own marketing analysis."
— TED TURNER

AS I MENTIONED earlier, one of my mentors as an adman was Darrin Stephens of *Bewitched* fame. Darrin not only had a magical wife, he had an incredible life. Creating snappy jingles and memorable slogans, he was exercising his brain. Less fortunate guys built up their biceps doing manual work. Samantha's husband built up his concepts by performing mental work. Come to think of it, Darrin possessed more magic than his bewitching wife. After all, he was being paid for his ideas. And the year was 1975. Yes, he was my beacon. Darrin Stephens was thinking for a living.

Two years later, I decided to do the same. It seemed like a good idea at the time. Advertising, at its worst, is justifiably ridiculed as an occupation that exalts the trivial and reduces everything — Japanese martial arts films, fine art, feminine hygiene products, toilet paper, Hamburger Helper, Spam, Tiffany's — to the level of products to be positioned, marketed, hawked, and sold. But at its best, advertising was and is one of the most creative of professions, a field where you're supposed to think for a living. In fact, at its best and its worst, advertising is a model of why ideas matter and how often our business structures go hopelessly awry.

I talk a lot about advertising in this book because it's the world I know best. But I also do it because there are few other occupations in which ideas play so central, inescapable, and critical a role. And though we think of it as being relatively modern, the advertising business has been around forever. In fact, I came up with a history of the world through the prism of advertising. It went like this:

ADVERTISING — THE FIRST MILLION YEARS

A little more than one million years ago, an artist watched a man battle a mean dinosaur. Returning to his cave, the artist sketched the scene on his wall. "Sportsman In Loincloth

Battling Triceratops," he titled it. Later that evening, over cocktails, his friends saw what was probably the world's first print ad.

Scholars refer to the period that followed as world history. I call it advertising in the making. And why not? It makes for great copy. In case you didn't know it, copywriting was actually invented in 3500 B.C. by the Sumerians. But it didn't catch on until 1800 B.C., when the first popular typeface appeared. It was called Canaanite — a precursor to the popular typeface, Helvetica Bold. Some years later, the world's first logo appeared — the Star of David; only to be followed by a catchy spin-off — the Christian crucifix. Soon, both logos led to "Thank God for God" bumper stickers and an ongoing competitive campaign between the two religions that was the inspiration for the Coke-Pepsi challenge. The battle also produced the industry's first memorable continuing character: the Pope.

Meanwhile, in 500 B.C., over tea at a Chinese restaurant, Confucius said, "Without knowing the force of words, it is impossible to know men." Presto! The philosophy of creative copywriting was born. Examples of the art can still be found in today's fortune cookies.

DYNAMITE IDEA

IN THE 1800s, ALFRED NOBEL MADE A FORTUNE WHEN HE INVENTED DYNAMITE AND OTHER EXPLOSIVES. HE TOOK THE MONEY AND LEFT IT IN A TRUST TO ESTABLISH PRIZES FOR PEACE, PHYSICS, CHEMISTRY, PHILOSOPHY, MEDICINE, AND LITERATURE, THUS CREATING THE NOBEL PEACE PRIZE.

Socrates won "Best of Show" the following spring. The assignment was a toughy: sell "contentment." His ad read: "Contentment is natural wealth, luxury is artificial poverty."

Two hundred years later, the world saw its first blockbuster campaign, created by Alexander the Great. Many of Alex's peers attributed his successes to excellent reach and frequency.

The next thousand years brought with them a creative drought. Sure, St. Paul and St. Augustine came up with a few memorable tag lines, and Genghis Khan went far with a hard-driving campaign, but no one seemed able to score with the Big Idea. Until A.D. 1300, that is, when a handful of pricey Italian boutiques launched the concept of the Renaissance. The art direction was "Clio" from day one. Print got a boost, too, from a guy named Gutenberg, who opened the world's first type house.

Then, in 1492, Columbus went international with the biggest idea since the Renaissance — untapped markets. And a decade later Leonardo da Vinci advanced the hottest new business theory to date: "If you don't have the product, invent it." It was rumored that da Vinci, Michelangelo, and Machiavelli would quit their respective agencies and join forces, but the heavy-hitting trio never got it together. Apparently, the two creatives came to believe that Machiavelli was looking out only for himself.

In the 1600s, Shakespeare made long copy respectable; Rembrandt walked away with all the art director awards; and Isaac Newton proved empirically that the oldest copy line in the universe — "What goes up must come down" — was effective against all target demos.

Halfway around the world, Ben Franklin lit up the industry when he and a bunch of account execs got together in Philadelphia to introduce a shaky new product: the U.S.A. Jefferson did the copywriting on the campaign, and Washington was management supervisor. Its unique selling propostion was "In God We Trust." The only trouble was the logo. Accounting wanted a turkey. Research said the crucifix had high awareness. Media suggested several symbols, one for each major demographic group. Finally, creative pitched the eagle "because it was bald." Nobody understood the rationale, but who were they to second-guess genius? Francis Scott Key was brought in to do the music, and the rest is history.

Back in Europe, Napoleon broke his own campaign with one of history's best-known mnemonics: the Man with His Hand in the Jacket. He hired Beethoven, of Bonn Music, to do the jingle; but after four submissions he fired the tunesmith, calling him "deaf." Beethoven turned around and sold his Fifth to Czar Alexander, who used it effectively to trash the French emperor's market share.

The battle, however, hardly compared to the clash of Blue versus Gray in the U.S. Civil War. Many considered the mud-slinging bad for the industry. Others said it was worth it because the United States came out "new and improved." Indeed, a decade later, some of America's greatest creative work appeared: Bell Reached Out and Touched Someone, Edison Brought Good Things to Life, and automobiles began to Build Excitement.

Meanwhile, Marconi claimed that radio was hot, Freud claimed that our ids were hot, and the Wright Brothers forced the advertising industry to double the per diem. Yet even Lenin and FDR, who made revolutionary breakthroughs in the field, couldn't match the biggest ad blitz of the century — The Third Reich. Armed with a powerful logo, excellent media placement, and hard-hitting creative, Hitler's campaign seemed destined to last a thousand years. There was only one hitch. The strategy of world domination through genocide turned off the public. And as we all know, if the strategy is wrong, the creative can't be right.

Once the air cleared following World War II, the industry discovered its most important tool since the caveman's flint stone: television. Unfortunately, though, TV's importance was reduced to three simple words: 15 percent commission.

The bottom line is this: Advertising has been around since the Beginning. God started it by creating man in His own "image."

GOD GETS OUT OF ADVERTISING

Advertising professionals believe that they are always making history. It's their nature. And frankly many of their advertising ideas have made a great impact. But I believe the industry has lost its way as it continues to look for more ways to create money instead of ideas.

Advertising agencies used to make a bundle of money by buying advertising space in print vehicles, radio programs, and television shows. But over time the business has unbundled itself. Today media is bought separately, as well as research and strategic planning, and now we're seeing that ideas can be marketed and purchased separately. To compensate, the ad guys have scrambled to cut costs, cut people, and cut time. The results have been horrifying. The world has become ad rich – six thousand media impressions a day — and idea poor.

It's not the fault of the people in advertising. Some are quite smart, but they're in a business that hasn't evolved enough to really reward, inspire, and foster its best ideas. Advertising agencies are constructed to manage clients, not ideas. Thinking, which takes time, costs money. So in the interest of a better bottom line, the system institutes deadlines. Not the chronological ones, but the fiscal stopwatch that says, "Stop already, we're running out of money."

The dismal result is that advertising agencies continue to crank out twenty-one thousand TV commercials a year — ads instead of ideas. Consumers are not dummies; they're very savvy. They want to invite the advertisers into their home, not have them break in. They want to make decisions, not have someone decide for them. As a result, consumer's are "zapping" more often, and advertisers are looking for a new alternative. Ads just aren't adding up anymore.

What is needed, then, is a new model for marketing — one that would be sensitive to the consumer and that would create and reward ideas, not just ads. The modern form of the advertising business, born in 1869 and dedicated the way few businesses are to the power of ideas, has become a very conservative business. It now kills more good ideas than it creates. If advertising, which is nothing without ideas, can't grow, sustain, and nurture ideas, what business can? That's why we need a big, new, idea-generating idea. And I think I've come up with one.

BRIGHTHOUSE, THE NEW PARADIGM

Few people think more than two or three times a year. I've made an international reputation for myself by thinking once or twice a week.
— GEORGE BERNARD SHAW

BrightHouse is my model for thinking. It is the world's first Ideation Corporation consisting of twenty-one people who think for a living. BrightHouse is the next step in the evolution toward a new millenium that will foster an explosion of ideas and creativity unlike anything we've seen before. The people who ignite our imaginations in the next century will become idea barons. Gray matter will be their real estate, and their net worth will be determined by what grows out of it.

BrightHouse has dimensionalized the thinking brain and built an office that works the same way. Our home is an old mansion peeking out among the tall, glass towers in Atlanta's top business district. We painted the exterior yellow, signifying the bright power of creativity, gutted the inside, and built a house that mirrors the creative process — where ideas are created in the east wing and take full form in the west wing, just as the sun rises in the east and sets in the west. The moldings of the house are festooned with quotations to remind ourselves and our clients of the primacy of the creative process. So the words of Albert Einstein above the conference table in what we call the incubation area read, "**Greatest ideas are often met with violent opposition from mediocre minds.**" In other parts of the building the moldings read, "**Leap and the net will appear**" and "**Creativity is intelligence having fun.**"

In as gentle and creative a way as we can, we have created, in effect, an assembly line of the mind. People don't come to work, they come to think.

We try to do everything differently from traditional advertising agencies, beginning with our fee structure. Clients pay for the idea, not its implementation or execution.

BrightHouse is the first company, then, fully compensated for its thinking process. We decide what we think our ideas and expertise are worth and charge accordingly.

It's an audacious idea, but so far it seems to be working. BrightHouse has created men's and

---

AN ALARMING IDEA

HAVE YOU EVER WONDERED WHO TO BLAME WHEN THE ALARM CLOCK GOES OFF? IF THE NAME JEAN EUGENE ROBERT HOUDIN DOESN'T RING A BELL IT'S BECAUSE HE WASN'T KNOWN AS AN INVENTOR BUT THE FOUNDER OF MODERN MAGIC. HIS PROTO-TYPE WOULD RING A BELL AS A LIGHTED CANDLE CAME OUT OF A BOX.

women's fragrances. We have changed the base-ball game experience through the groundbreaking environment we helped create at the Atlanta Braves' Turner Field. We have changed blue-chip companies' cultures. We have created new vistas in marketing. And we are educating America to the death of the brand and the birth of the bond. Our work has touched societies as far away as China and Singapore and has hit as close to home as the 1996 Atlanta Olympics.

Our clients are the world's top chief executives, the men and women who not only have visions but also control destinies for their companies. It is through their eyes that we can see into the hearts and minds of tomorrow's customer, and what we've seen is clear. Ideas rule. I'm not going to tell you that everyone can start a successful idea company. But I will tell you that if your company, whether it sells underwear or software, doesn't realize that ideas are the core of its business, then you're in big trouble. Which is why my story is about a lot more than advertising.

And where do those ideas come from? How does one incubate them? Exactly how does one go about thinking for a living? That's what the next chapter is all about.

CHAPTER 4

SOCRATES, MCLUHAN, CSIKSZENTMIHALYI, AND ME: A BRIEF HISTORY OF THINKING

"In art there are only two types of people: revolutionaries and plagiarists."
— GAUGUIN

IT'S NO BIG surprise that the Original Idea, according to the scriptures, was light. Light removed the darkness, and ever since God turned on the lights, people have been thinking.

One could say that the first idea came from a woman. After all, Eve ate the apple — the fruit of knowledge. This caused her to be self-conscious. Adam quickly followed, and the fall began. Still others choose Abraham, who took dictation from God to help create the Bible, probably the greatest display of big ideas ever compiled.

Aristotle might actually have created the first model of thinking when he divided the psyche into knowing, striving, and feelings, but

Aristotle learned from Homer who penned *The Iliad* and *The Odyssey*. These works offer us an enormous amount to think about. Where did Homer's ideas come from? Mark Twain wrote in a letter to Helen Keller, "All ideas are second-hand, consciously or unconsciously drawn from a million outside sources and used by the garnerer with pride and satisfaction."

The Talmudic Model of the Bible actually has a square in it where the sages have written their thoughts. Around the square are more squares with comments from rabbis throughout the ages. These teachers are commenting upon commentary suggesting that knowledge is cumulative through discussion. This is a terrific model for thought because it asks the question, "Who is a wise person?" It answers, "One who learns from all people."

Socrates might be the first idea man whose ideas were actually valued because he never wrote or painted a thing! Thanks to Plato, Socrates' thinking has been quoted throughout time. The fact that Socrates could neither read nor write is proof of the incredible power and impact of pure thought. He never picked up a pen or brush, but his thinking changed the world.

IDEAS DEMAND A LEAP

IN THE 1800s THERE LIVED A FRENCH AERIALIST WHOSE FIRST NAME WAS JULES. LOOKING FOR A MORE COMFORTABLE GAR-MENT TO WEAR WHILE PERFORMING HIS SOMERSAULTS ON THE FLYING TRAPEZE, HE CREATED THE "LEOTARD." THAT WAS ALSO HIS LAST NAME.

I'm certainly not the first person who tried to think for a living. Montaigne wrote in an essay that "thinking is living." John H. McMurphy, author of *Secrets from Great Minds*, tells us that Sir Isaac Newton gazed at the heavens for hours, often entering a dreamstate. It was in the stars that he found his way. Beethoven took long walks. Percy Shelley sat by the lake, Leonardo da Vinci stared at cracked floors, and William Wordsworth gazed at the fireplace as ideas crackled in his mind. These idea people gave their work an enormous amount of thought. Their thinking created ideas that inspired and changed the world.

McMurphy suggests that almost without exception these thinkers developed techniques to alter their state of mind so that they could pick up some universal creative inspiration. The office where people think for a living is the world and beyond. Mother Teresa, certainly one of our civilization's most compassionate thinkers, said that she was "a little pencil in God's hand." I've always believed that **creativity is a state of mind, not the state you live in.** Making sense of that state has perplexed greater minds than mine for centuries. But, in fact, a brief history of thinking does provide some remarkably consistent ideas about how we think and how we can do it better. All thinkers are inspired to think. They are passionate in their pursuit of truth. Thinkers persevere to points of obsession, and they believe that the solution is theirs before they begin their thinking journeys. As for how we can think better, most great thinkers will tell you that's the secret, to believe that it can be done better.

My First Model of Thinking

Fantasy was my earliest experiment in thinking. Imagining a tiger as a pet was my first recollection. During a show-and-tell class at Columbia Grammar School in New York City, I brought in a can of Tiger's Milk. The name, of course, was the brand-name and had nothing to do with tigers. Actually, it was a dietary supplement that had found its way into the Reiman family's cupboard.

Nonetheless, show-and-tell was an arena in which to show and tell what you were most excited about, so I told my first-grade peers, over milk, that Tiger's Milk made you stronger and taller and smarter. I should know. After all, my tiger lived at home in my bedroom. He weighed a thousand pounds, and no one could see him except me. The reason, as I explained, was that my wall was painted with stripes so my tiger's would blend in.

My teacher was unimpressed and called my parents to say that I had disturbed the other kids in the class. Today, I realize I had altered their shared reality, which is pretty admirable at the age of six, even if it seemed deplorable to my teacher.

Picasso often said that he reached his peak at eight years of age and spent the next seventy years trying to recapture that creativity. Thinking, at its most creative, recaptures the serendipitous brilliance of children, but some great minds over time have tried to make sense of just how the process works. I've tried to learn from as many of them as I could and then construct my own model of how the creative process works.

THE ORIGINAL THINKER

We could go back further, but let's start our history of thinking with one Hermann von Helmholtz. Our boy Hermann graduated from the Medical Institute in Berlin in 1843 and was assigned to a military regiment at Potsdam, but he spent all his time doing research. He later became a professor of anatomy, physiology, and physics. Sounds like a thinker to me.

During his seventy-three years of life, he became interested in *the anatomy of thinking*. He became the first person to categorize his own creativity in terms of specific stages. The first was *saturation*, or the gathering of information and data. The second was *incubation*, when all the data was sifted through and thought about. The third was *illumination*, in which the *Aha!* or breakthrough happened. In 1908, the French mathematician Henri Poincaré added a fourth stage called *verification*. It was here that the *Aha!* idea was tested and validated.

A little more than one hundred years later, psychologist Graham Wallis, author of *The Art of Thought*, created his thinking model. Wallis broke down creativity into a four-step process he defined as follows:

1. Preparation
2. Incubation
3. Illumination
4. Verification

1. In the *preparation* stage, we define the problem, need, or desire, and gather any information.

We also set up criteria for verifying the solution's acceptability.

2. In the *incubation* stage, we step back from the problem and let our minds contemplate and work it through. Like preparation, incubation can last minutes, weeks, even years.

3. In the *illumination* stage, ideas arise from the mind to provide the basis of a creative response. These ideas can be pieces of the whole itself, that is, seeing the entire concept or entity all at once. Unlike the other stages, illumination is often very brief, involving a tremendous rush of insights within a few minutes or hours.

4. In *verification*, the final stage, we carry out activities to demonstrate whether or not what emerged in illumination satisfies the need and meets the criteria defined in the preparation stage.

A variety of writers and psychologists have massaged Helmhotz's model of creativity, including American psychologist Jacob Getzels, who added *discovery*. This is the revelation that puts the process in motion.

THE CSIKSZENTMIHALYI MODEL FOR CREATIVITY

Perhaps the leading authority on creativity is the author Mihaly Csikszentmihalyi, who wrote *Creativity: Flow and the Psychology of Discovery and Invention.* Clearly, anyone who can spell Csikszentmihalyi is no mental slouch. He added an extraordinarily important element to the research and theorizing on thinking — his recognition that creativity is inseparable from context. Ideas are as much a product and reflection of the existing world as an advance from it. Csikszentmihalyi says that creativity requires both a context (the domain) and an audience (the judges). In his view, raw talent is less essential to creativity than a rich domain and receptive judges, because these inspire and reward creativity. That helps explain why certain eras — the Renaissance is a great example — foster extraordinary leaps forward in human creativity. People didn't suddenly get smarter or more talented. What changed was the field — the sociocultural environment in which they lived that suddenly provided ways to fund, nurture, spark, and reward creativity.

WHERE IS WHERE BIG IDEAS COME FROM

Csikszentmihalyi asks the question, "Where is creativity?" as opposed to, "What is creativity?" By doing so, he expands our notion of creativity in a very profound way. Instead of a mysterious spark of genius found within individuals, Csikszentmihalyi saw a dynamic interplay of individual and environment, between a single person trying to create new ideas and a context that either helped or thwarted him or her.

Csikszentmihalyi created a triangle based on three areas: (1) domain, (2) individual talent, and (3) judges. In effect, all creative ideas are mediated, evaluated, rewarded, valued, or devalued by the domain — the broader field in which it plays out — and by judges, those with the power to pass judgment and hand out rewards and penalties. Csikszentmihalyi also explored the concept of flow — the intense feeling of excitement and creativity that comes from focused effort and that fosters creative surges. He looked at flow both in terms of individual dynamics and in terms of the broader society. The result again was a dynamic notion of creativity as something constantly shifting and evolving in which what happened at the individual level and what happened at the societal level were intimately linked. I'll come back to Dr. C. later in the book, but the critical idea to remember here is **the link between individual and domain**. It's why thinking for a living is a notion that's as important to all of us collectively as it is to each of us individually.

THE MARSHALL MCLUHAN MODEL

Marshall McLuhan was never known as an architect of thinking models, but he was a visionary thinker. He was actually an English professor who communicated above all the amazing wonder of the thinking mind. Most of us know media guru McLuhan because of the popularity of his statement, "The medium is the message." However, he said something else that has become one of my business mantras and should be included in your toolbox for creative thinking.

> Everybody experiences far more than he understands. Yet it is experience, rather than understanding, that influences behavior.

This model begs the question, What is more important — understanding or the experience? To illustrate the answer, consider the following two approaches to the same challenge.

THE UNDERSTANDING

Make believe you own a museum. You desperately want people to visit your dinosaur exhibit. To create traffic, you advertise your exhibition by showing a skeleton of a Tyrannosaurus Rex that was discovered in Minsk, Russia, under a mile of molten rock and meticulously excavated and reconstructed by paleontologists at enormous cost. Unfortunately, after one short stare, families leave understanding dinosaurs but unscathed by a million years of evolution and the faceless jaws hovering fourteen stories above.

THE EXPERIENCE

Across the street is the Dinosaur Experience. In the lobby is a T-Rex made by a model maker for $1,000. Its jaws are the size of six children's heads. And instead of a security guard, a museum photographer records your child's face as he sticks his head inside the sound-designed, gnashing jaws,

---

McIDEA

As founder of the McDonald's Corporation, Ray Kroc revolutionized the restaurant industry when he opened his first McDonald's in 1955. His big idea regarding customer service has been the model for countless companies around the world. And his Big Mac is pretty good, too.

imagining what it would be like if, instead of coming here for lunch, he came here as dinner. Conventional advertising, that is, giving the consumer only information, is as extinct as the dinosaur at Experiential Marketing is the future.

Museums will not be the only benefactors of experiential marketing. All retailers today are looking for new ways to create meaningful experiences with their customers. They know that conventional advertising is not enough. Lazy marketing creates a monologue with customers while an experience creates a dialogue.

A good example of a retail experience is the one we created for the Metropolitan Museum of Art stores. To attract the whole family to the store, we simulated an archeological dig. The plan called for a twenty-four-inch deep hole to be cut in the retailer's floor, just big enough to hold a television set. The image on the screen would be a real archeological dig, giving the impression that it was much deeper. We would then rope off the dig and let kids and parents witness a real excavation.

An example of experiential marketing that you might be more familiar with is Niketown. Walking into this multidimensional sports arena and buying a $140 pair of shoes is just part of the experiential shopping experience. Bass Pro Shops lure shoppers by offering them the opportunity to cast into a test pool before dropping their dollars on a fishing rod. MARS: Music And Recording Superstore invites customers to try out guitars or record a demo before buying a musical instrument. They also offer music lessons. The company is rocking and rolling with a goal of sixty superstores. REI, a Seattle-based chain of stores that sells camping equipment, installed a sixty-four-foot clay wall that people can climb. After their ascent, shoppers can test a Gortex jacket in a simulated rainstorm. Executives found that these interactive experiences made the stores hugely successful.

The Internet is the newest entry into experiential marketing because it is interactive. Eventually, all companies will realize that experiential ideas are worth more to a company than advertising.

In some respects experiential marketing is just as important as operational efficiency. For instance, the Ford Motor Company is putting more money into dealerships than ever before, because they know that the customers' experience is more important than customers understanding what's under the hood.

It's clear that experiences rather than mere images are extraordinarily powerful in changing consumers' behavior. These events create bonds with people who are looking to experience life rather than just understand it. As the great Joseph Campbell wrote, "People say that what we're all seeking is the meaning of life. . . . I think that what we're really seeking is an experience of being alive."

Unfortunately, our education system has failed to teach experientially. Most of us were taught to memorize as opposed to learn through experience. Most of us know why the "chicken crossed the road," but we don't know how he got there. When I went to school, I was told to memorize three chapters by Friday. Today many children are being taught experientially. That is, many of their CD-ROM interactive programs take them through a series of steps that are neither right nor wrong. All of them, however, have different consequences. The experience is interactive.

> *Adventure is something you seek for pleasure, or even for profit, like a gold rush invading a country. But experience is what really happens to you in the long run; the truth that finally overtakes you.*
> — KATHERINE ANNE PORTER,
> American novelist

We will see later how experiencing the details of life creates life's colorful portrait and how changing education and enhancing the power of ideas in society go hand in hand. If creativity is one's output, then experience is the input.

THE REIMAN MODEL

I'm not Marshall McLuhan, and I doubt I could make it through life if I had to stop and remember how to spell Csikszentmihalyi a few times a day, but I've tried to learn from them and many others. And what I've tried to do in my career and now in my business is to take their insights and put them together into my own unified theory of creativity. My recipe includes a variation of Wallis's four steps, pieces of the McCluhan Experiential Model, and Csikszentmihalyi's model of *where* creativity is as opposed to *what* it is. I stress *where* because, like Csikszentmihalyi, I am keenly aware that in the world of marketing, creativity is not a *what* but rather an interactive dialogue among (1) talented minds, (2) the domain of marketing, and (3) the ultimate judges — the consumers. To that mixture I add one final ingredient, a touch of divine intervention, and the result is BrightHouse, a living, creative thought process *where* great experiential ideas are created.

THE CREATIVE PROCESS OF IDEATION

Like Wallis, I've come up with four stages of creativity. Only my model is not just a road map to how great thoughts evolve. It's a business. That is to say, I have taken the thinking process and built a working organization around it that processes problems very much in the same way as Wallis imagined. The four stages, or four I's, are:

1. Investigation
2. Incubation
3. Illumination
4. Illustration

Our staff's goal at BrightHouse is the *Journey of Ideation*. Over a six-week period we take on the roles of the investigator, the incubator, the illuminator, and the illustrator. The result is *The Big Idea*.

THE FOUR I'S™

INVESTIGATION
Investigation is the first stage of the ideation process. During this time, we deploy strategic detectives who gather and analyze qualitative and quantitative data to create the BrightHouse Branding Blueprint℠. This map is studied by a

coterie of world-class experts, gleaned from various disciplines. For example, we might have the world's leading color theorist discuss the power, perception, and impact of the color red for a Coca-Cola project. Or we might have a scientist create a patent for a paint that creates a pleasant scent year round. Psychologists, professors, and even priests have offered their perspectives during investigation. These specialists bring their unique insights and perspectives to the BrightHouse Ideation Model. This exploration is augmented by a systematic inquiry of our client's senior management, which ultimately leads to the destiny statement for the company or project.

INCUBATION

The best way to create a high-*quality* idea is to create a high-*quantity* of ideas. And the best way to do this is to think. Thinking takes time, so the longest stage of the ideation process is incubation.

With our strategic framework now in place, we allow our minds to go out and play. Individually, the BrightHouse staff begins blending its ideas with others, juxtaposing them, turning them inside out, upside down, and examining them either verbally or visually by creating an adlike object or picture and pinning it to the wall. The staff will come together often to brainstorm and to attempt to create an idea or experience that, as Steven Jobs says, "would make a dent in the universe." In a series of exercises, which range from meditation to going to the movies, thinkers experiment and discover ideas, images, and approaches. What we want is the one elusive image, insight, idea, or approach that will provide a level of clarity and insight that will separate it from all the others.

Conventional corporate structures prohibit employees from thinking properly because they penalize them for incubation. This dilemma started in school when teachers handed out pink slips for daydreaming. But dreaming during waking hours is essential to the thinking process. What's more, without daydreaming you're highly unlikely to have an illustration or *Aha!* experience. To daydream is to begin to understand.

When I was an employee for a number of large advertising agencies, I was encouraged to be fast, not slow. There's nothing wrong with speed. But if I spent time thinking instead of writing, I was often the target of jests. "Where are you?" "Are you alright?" "Did someone hypnotize you?" "Big lunch, huh?"

Daydreaming is at the heart of BrightHouse. Our belief is that the act of daydreaming, or what we prefer to call incubation, creates unheard of and unthought of possibilities. By turning our company into a Think Pad, we get results no one else can.

Every BrightHouse project entails three weeks of incubation. This includes blending, exploring, juxtaposing, traveling, polarizing, reinforcing, walking, talking, meditating, meeting experts, brainstorming, praying, and sharing epiphanies. Out of this creative ferment comes hundreds of ideas ready to be edited.

CHARLIE CHAPLIN
DEFINES GENIUS

The comic genius Charlie Chaplin defined genius as "the ability to edit." It's true. Quantity begets quality. If you want to find the answer, ask as many questions as possible.

ILLUMINATION

Big ideas don't appear, they evolve. Therefore, stage three edits stage two. The nucleus of BrightHouse is its diversified management team, made up of strategic specialists and creative conceptualists. It is here, however, that they all have one common purpose — illuminate the Big Idea or have the *Aha!* experience. This is the moment of brilliance, the moment when all the pieces come together in a flash.

How do you know when you've got the Big Idea? The rule is: When someone thinks they have the Big Idea, they are usually correct. The tell-tale sign of a great idea is that almost everyone around you thinks it's great. Hopefully, it's an idea that will dent the universe. Once discovered, the idea is honed, checked for strategic synchronicity, given an identity, and run through a stringent series of legal due diligence.

The *Aha!* or Big Idea or corporate epiphany is the illumination every great thinker seeks. That's because it's both the culmination of intense think-

---

BIGGEST IDEA IN THE WORLD

CONFUCIUS WAS BORN IN 551 B.C. AND WAS CHINA'S MOST FAMOUS TEACHER AND PHILOSOPHER. UNABLE TO OBTAIN AN OFFICIAL POSITION IN HIS STATE, HE SPENT HIS LIFE SHARING IDEAS WITH HIS DISCIPLES. HIS TEACHINGS, KNOWN AS *The Analects*, HAVE BECOME THE BASIS OF SOCIAL LIFESTYLE IN CHINA, KOREA, JAPAN, AND INDOCHINA. THIS MIGHT MAKE HIM THE BIGGEST IDEA MAN IN THE WORLD.

ing and also a new piece of intellectual property. In today's business game, the *Aha!* has replaced the hotel on Monopoly's Boardwalk. It is valuable, touchable, enviable, and transferable. That is, today's unique idea is money in the bank.

Few chief executives dispute the strategic value of an *Aha!*, but many leaders don't know what to do with one when they get it. Ideas are still run up the flagpole to see whether they fly. This is a mistake because the chief executive is relying on the winds of change rather than being the change itself. Top executives are judged by how they fly in a storm. Sunny days are for picnics. Likewise, great ideas can take off regardless of the corporate weather.

Ahas! are not meant to be managed, they are created to manage. *Ahas!* are the visions that move companies forward. Therefore, they are priceless to people at the helms of their companies.

ILLUSTRATION

The purpose of illustration is to visually portray and personify the Big Idea. Through a series of applications, which range from advertising and design to Experiential Marketing^{SM} and new communication paradigms, we put together a creative and strategic plan for our client in oral and written form. The Big Idea is now ready to move out of BrightHouse and into the marketplace.

BrightHouse is only the first experiment in *Thinkonomics* — the value raw thinking will have on the marketplace. Today, however, it proves that a business can be built around the process of thinking. What's more, it's proof that corporate visionaries want and need ideas and are prepared to pay for them.

As the world becomes more computerized and digitalized, original thinking will be idolized. As intuitive and unfinished as BrightHouse is, it is a harbinger of the U.S. business model of the future. This little house could open the doors for a new way to think about your career, your business, and life.

4 I's C > 2

So what's the bottom line? I summarize in the following formula, even though I was no whiz at math: 4 I's C > 2.

Four I's see greater than two eyes is my equation for living, loving, and working, not just marketing. In every facet of life we seem to be compromising the four parts that make up life itself. Investigating life means more than slowing down to smell the roses. It means stopping and examining the roses. Having a genuine encounter with life makes the experience of living richer and allows us to truly give birth to ourselves. Incubating is a lot like meditating. It's what the flip side of prayer is all about. When you pray, you talk to God. When you meditate, you listen to God. Illuminations are the *Aha's!* Nothing feels like them, but you can't have a full illumination until you've taken the time to investigate and incubate. And finally there's illustration. Until there is shape to an idea, there is no substance. **That is why the greatest repository of ideas are graveyards.** Here ideas remain buried with the people who had them but did nothing with them.

A society of thinkers is worlds apart from where we are today. Today, many of us are paid *not* to think. In schools, the answer has always been more important than the thought process. At work, we're encouraged to find the solution ASAP (if the *S* stood for slow we'd have something here). At home we've created something called *quality* time, when what is really needed is *quantity* time. The best illustration of a nonthinking society is our military, where people are paid not to think but to take orders.

The marketplace will change. Ideas will reveal their power. In their wake will be left the anachronistic organization of mill managers overseeing run-of-the-mill people. Tomorrow, the managers' subordinates will be smarter than the managers. Supervisors will regulate the thinking process to keep it healthy as well as wealthy. Companies will create living libraries — groups of experts that provide a constant stream of knowledge to fellow employees. Our careers will turn into individual companies as our minds and ideas become increasingly valuable. Every home will have a sanctuary where families can think, meditate, and listen. Schools will encourage our students to play with a problem as opposed to working at it. First, however, the picture of how we value ideas must change.

ARTISTS NEED NOT PAINT THEMSELVES INTO A CORNER

One day art galleries will commission artists to paint instead of collecting commissions on their paintings. This is what I tell my mother-in-law and fine artist, Marinoff. Like other recognized painters, she believes that being shown in the right gallery signifies success.

These galleries may serve the struggling artists, but to the semiestablished painter, they create a grim picture. To these artists, they send the clear message: "Unless you're hanging in here, hang it up." This threat, in turn, threatens the artists' value, not just on the street, but in their own minds.

I know many successful artists who sell their works to collectors. Both parties believe they have received enormous value. Artists who believe in their own self-worth will have a much greater canvas on which to paint. Galleries are less important when you establish your own value.

Having a gallery represent artists is only a brush with fame. They don't guarantee perpetuity or wealth. Only the artist's work can do that. Artists who are both talented and passionate will be successful, but the artist who passionately believes in herself possesses the greatest talent of all. She is successful already.

FROM BLUE CHIPS TO GOLDEN IDEAS

The world has so many thinkers to admire, but how many of these people have been financially rewarded?

Upon taking some money out of the ATM the other day, it struck me that the man who thought up the ATM probably never saw a penny from that idea. Artists rarely see the profit from their genius. But the world of ideas is changing, and the result will be that the ideators will not be shortchanged.

In *Blur*, written by Christopher Meyer and Stan Davis, both men agree, "Brains are the economy's most valuable resource." What they add is the insight that "We have no financial markets to trade in them." Here's my favorite part: "One of the major new financial instruments will involve the securitization of individuals." So get ready to invest in the idea people. Get ready for the people stock exchange where corporate and individual investors will invest in individuals. One day we will see golden ideas replace blue-chip companies. That is, there will be a virtual idea exchange among countries, cultures, and peoples. One idea building upon another to create yet a better one.

However, before we can change the world we need to change our minds. Almost twenty-five years ago, on a dark road in Rome, Italy, I had a change of mind and an experience that changed my life forever. From my darkest experience, I learned an amazing amount about how bright thoughts create light and about the limitless potential of the human mind.

VITAMIN 'I'

THE NEXT TIME YOU FEEL LIKE YOU'RE IN A "FUNK," REMEMBER FUNK IS THE NAME OF THE MAN WHO COINED THE WORD *vitamin*. THOUGH CASMIR FUNK BASED MANY OF HIS FINDINGS ON OTHER SCIENTISTS' WORK, HIS CONTRIBUTIONS REVOLUTIONIZED BIOCHEMISTRY AND MEDICINE, NOT TO MENTION HIS IDEA OF LISTING M.D.A., OR MINIMUM DAILY ALLOWANCE, ON CEREAL BOXES.

CHAPTER 5

How the Scariest Experience of My Life Taught Me That Thinking Is About a Lot More Than Thought

*"Faith is believing in that in which you
have not seen. The reward of faith is
seeing that in which you believed."*
— St. Augustine

WHEN YOU'RE LYING in a hospital bed thousands of miles from your home and a million miles from your dream, you have a lot of time to think. That's where I found myself in July 1975 following what I took to be the worst experience of my life — a terrifying car wreck along the Via Veneto in Rome. My upper arm bone, the humerus, was crushed, resulting in a devastating paralysis of the radial nerve and my right hand.

The prognosis was bleak. In a moment, I went from a twenty-two-year-old would-be filmmaker who would study under the great director Federico Fellini, a kid on top of the world, to a very scared little boy, staring up at a crucifix that looked down upon me and dozens of ailing men in a dingy hospital bed in Italy, wondering whether I'd ever be able to use a pen again.

But from that frightening episode, I learned a lesson that's empowered me ever since. I learned about the awesome power of faith that we all have within us. I learned, in essence, how to think — not in terms of the science of cognition, but in terms of the magic of the human mind. Everything I know about thinking, about the power of the mind to create amazing things and work odd and miraculous wonders, comes out of that experience. I figured out that the way back to health boiled down to a simple but amazingly powerful thought — if I could get my thumb up, the rest of my body would follow.

Physicians have told me that it takes nineteen days to create a habit. So, I had to think and act for at least nineteen days, believing that my thumb, followed by my hand, was going to

---

NOBEL IDEA

"EXAMPLE IS NOT THE MAIN THING IN INFLUENCING OTHERS. IT IS THE ONLY THING," WROTE NOBEL PEACE PRIZE WINNER ALBERT SCHWEITZER. AFTER BECOMING A DOCTOR AND SURGEON, HE MOVED TO AFRICA AND BUILT A HOSPITAL. HE LATER SET UP A LEPER COLONY. HIS BIG IDEA WAS HUMAN SERVICE. "DO SOMETHING FOR SOMEBODY EVERY DAY FOR WHICH YOU DO NOT GET PAID," HE ADVISED.

move. First the thought, then the action, then the habit. That was a very big revelation for a scared kid lying in an Italian hospital room, one that I've never forgotten. It means to me that in the beginning was the Idea. Maybe it's the idea for a new product, or a new way to make your marriage work, or a new way to teach your kids how to experience joy. Maybe it's a new management structure for your company, a new way to get yourself to exercise, or a new thought on how to keep to your diet. But what I realized is that **you are what you think**, and whatever you create is a personification, a dimensionalization of your thoughts.

What I designed for myself was an enormous exercise in empowering, creative thinking. Night after night I would lie in that bed and pray. I would think about what was really important — that I was alive, and I wanted to make the most of every moment of my life. I've often told people to check their birth certificate and to imagine the number 700,000 is in the corner of your birth certificate. That's your net worth — the amount of hours the average person has to live, and how you invest those hours is completely up to you. In that hospital bed, I invested all my energy into a single thought: If I could get my thumb up, I'd be OK. In the end, I got my thumb up, I got my hand back, I got my future back, and I came up with a simple road map for living and thinking that I consider one of my best ideas.

I turned that idea into my book *Success: The Original Handbook*, which begins with the thought that wisdom is at our fingertips. I began by being thumbs-up, being positive, remembering that thoughts have wings, and that motions lead to emotions. The real value is self-worth, not net worth.

The pointer finger teaches us to always point at what we want. It's also a reminder that one of the most rewarding things in life is getting rid of what you don't need. Most people think they need more — but the truth is they really need less. They need to be simpler. They need to get back to what makes them tick. They need to point toward what they really need and really want so they have focus and direction.

The middle finger, of course, carries an indelicate message, but it can be an empowering one. The point of the third finger is to give the finger to fear. Fear is an illusion — don't take life so seriously. None of us is going to get out alive. So the important thing is to learn to laugh at our fears, to ridicule them, to give them the finger, and to move past them.

The fourth finger is about marching forth. The best revenge is to move forward. When ice cream is on your plate, eat it! Enjoy. The fourth finger is why I give all my employees the day off on March 4 every year, so they can remember that thoughts have to be turned into actions and that to succeed one has to set a course and march forth toward it. This year I intend to go to a greeting card company with the idea of *National Marching Forth Day*. One card might say, "Don't take the day off. Take the day on. Happy March 4th!"

And finally, there's the little finger to remind us that the little things in life can make a big dif-

ference, and it's the small gestures, small kind-
nesses, small insights that can lead to much bigger things. Emerson said, "The creation of a
thousand forests is in one acorn," and I always
try to remember that every great dream and
great achievement is made up of hundreds of little ones, every great relationship is made up of
many small hugs, small gestures, and intimate
words. God is in the details, and if we don't get
the little things right, we'll never get the big
ones.

What I learned in that hospital bed, and what
I found in the palm of my hand, was the tanta-
lizing interplay between thought and spirit,
between specific ideas and a general way of
looking at the world. Indeed, when I look at
some of my best ideas and some of the things
that most motivated me over the years, I'm
struck by how much they're about the intangibles of spirit and sensibility rather than about
the machinations of intellect.

Take, for instance, the importance of *passion*.
One reason I'm able to think for a living is
because I've been so passionate about my work,
so invested in the notion that anything is possible, that I've taken risks that might have seemed
crazy at the time but paid off big in the end.

Many years ago when I was pitching the Del
Taco business, I was pitted against one of the
largest advertising agencies in the world. I was
one of the smallest. But my ideas, which were
fired by passion and enthusiasm, made me bigger.

Here's what happened. Both advertising agencies made their presentations. The next day I
called the chairman of the board to ask how we

did. The chairman said, "You did a fabulous job." I asked, "How was my creativity?" He said it was brilliant. I asked, "How was my research?" He said it was thorough. I asked, "How was my account service lineup . . . I mean, are my people good?" He said, "They're the best." I asked, "Well, how did the other agency do?" He said, "Well, they did the same, and whoever wins this, it's going to be a win-win for the Del Taco organization."

That's just what I didn't want to hear. I wanted him to say I was going to win. I went home, and I started thinking. I'd already given him my best ideas. But suddenly I realized that the best idea of all was not an idea that would be on TV or radio, but an idea that would reach his heart and prove to him that mine was the agency for the job.

Del Taco was in Dallas, and I was in Atlanta, but I figured if I could find out where the top company officials would be eating that week, I could make a final, decisive pitch for the account.

Through a little investigative work, I found out that the chairman, the president, and the executive vice president in charge of marketing and sales were eating at Casa Mia, a beautiful, upscale, Mexican restaurant in Dallas. So I went to a wonderful Mexican restaurant in Atlanta called Rio Bravo, where I've had many margaritas over the years, and I presented the mariachi band with a modest proposal.

I hired the Rio Bravo mariachi band and put them on a plane to Dallas. Once there, I sent them to Casa Mia, paid off the maitre'd, and got him to put my mariachi band in and take his mariachi band out. While the Del Taco chairman, president, and marketing director dined, and while I watched from a nearby table, the counterfeit mariachis began singing, "Ay, yay, yay, yay . . . hire Babbit & Reiman." And they went on for another half hour literally singing the praises of my agency. When it was over, the mariachis and I flew back to Atlanta, and I went back to my office.

At the time, my agency was on the tenth floor, and the satellite office of the gorilla agency I was competing against was on the twentieth floor, the penthouse of the same building. Well, at eleven o'clock the phone rang. It was the chairman of the board of Del Taco. He said, "Mr. Reiman, are you sitting on the west side of the building?" I said, "Yes, sir, I am." He said, "Look outside your window." And outside my window, hovering maybe twenty yards away from me, was a helicopter. The helicopter turned 180 degrees, and written across the side of it was "Congratulations, Joey. You won." It was my confirmation that one person with passion is a majority, and that some of the most creative thinking in the world is the kind that touches the heart, not just the mind. The chairman on the phone said, "Is there anything we can do at this early time in our relationship? You've shown such great enthusiasm for us." And I said, "Yes, sir, there is. Could you have your helicopter pilot hover up about ten flights?"

I did some good thinking to get that account. But without the passion to go the extra mile, to risk looking like an utter fool, none of the big thoughts would have amounted to anything.

One of my favorite quotes is from President Teddy Roosevelt. He said, "Far better it is to dare mighty things that are checkered by failure, than to live in the gray twilight that knows not victory nor defeat." I tried to paraphrase that quote, and I came up with "The safe way is a grocery store." The fact of the matter is that no matter what we are given, whatever hand we are dealt, *to think creatively we must think positively.*

Demosthenes, who was a great speaker, stuttered. Caesar, the great statesman, was an epileptic. Ben Franklin was poor in his pocket but certainly not in his mind or his heart. Cézanne was rejected from art school. Churchill had learning disabilities. And Reiman had his right hand paralyzed. Not such a tall order. But for me it was very, very important to get that hand moving. It taught me the tenets of creativity: being positive, being focused, taking action. It wasn't enough to be positive, focused, and fearless, I had to take action! Musicians say that the hardest part of practicing is taking the instrument out of the case. To begin is to be half done! This is what we need to do with our ideas. And how do you create great ideas? How do you make them really happen? By taking action on them. Action is the great separator. It separates the rich from the poor, the winners from the whiners, and the ideas from the "I did its." Action gets things done.

Equally important as the **passion** to take action is the **persistence** to see it through. The world is full of people with good ideas, but often the difference between those who achieve great success and those who don't is the persistence to overcome obstacles, resistance, and rejections.

There's an instructional story about a guy who failed at business at the age of thirty-two, was defeated at a legislative race at thirty-two, and then failed in business again at thirty-four. But he didn't really mind because he was so in love with this woman. If you read their letters, you'd get diabetes because they were so sweet. And then she died. She died two months before their planned wedding. He had a nervous breakdown and was institutionalized, but when he got out he went right back to politics. And still his bad luck continued. He lost election after election. He lost congressional races. He lost a Senate race. He tried to become vice president and failed at that, too. His whole life was strewn with setbacks, but he had enormous tenacity and he was on fire with ideas, and he knew that if he did not follow his dream, those ideas would be buried alive. So at the age of fifty-six he ran one more time. For one more office. This time it paid off, so big, in fact, that today you'll find him on a $5 bill. Abraham Lincoln became President.

If you want the fruit, you have to go out on a limb. If you want to hit the jackpot, you've got to put the coin in the machine. Live now. Create

---

MOST VISIONARY IDEA

SHE COULDN'T SEE, HEAR, OR SPEAK, YET HELEN KELLER COMMUNICATED MORE COURAGE, FAITH, AND OPTIMISM THAN ANYONE OF HER TIME. HER BIG IDEA WAS TRANSCENDING PHYSICAL HANDICAPS. AND SO SHE DID, GRADUATING CUM LAUDE FROM RADCLIFFE COLLEGE IN 1904. AS SHE PUT IT, "LIFE IS EITHER A DARING ADVENTURE OR NOTHING."

now. People who keep one foot in the past and one foot in the future always end up peeing on the present.

I was out the other night with my children, Alden and Julien, four and two, and we saw some fireflies. I remembered that fireflies light up only when they move forward. There's a similar light that goes off in my mind when I'm trying to create. I know I need to be positive. I need to remove the fear. I need to stay focused and concentrate. I need to take action. As Helen Keller said, "Life is a daring adventure or nothing." We all need to become verbs, not nouns.

And we need to remember that sometimes God's schedule is not ours, that things take time, that ideas and thoughts need to **percolate** before they reach fruition. The world is full of great truisms that turn out to be false and impossible ideas that turn out to be gloriously, triumphantly doable after all. Consider, for a moment, the following quotations:

"Everything that can be invented has been invented."

— CHARLES H. DUELL
Director of U.S. Patent Office, 1899

"Who the hell wants to hear actors talk?"
— HARRY WARNER
Warner Brothers Pictures, 1927

"Sensible and responsible women do not want to vote."
— GROVER CLEVELAND, 1905

"There is no likelihood man can ever tap the power of the atom."
— ROBERT MILLIKAN
Nobel Prize in Physics, 1923

"Heavier than air flying machines are impossible."
— LORD KELVIN
President, Royal Society, 1835

The visionaries who saw beyond the conventional wisdom didn't succeed overnight. But they wouldn't have succeeded at all if they didn't know that good thoughts and good works take time to grow and mature, and that today's sense of what's possible can be tomorrow's foolish footnote to history.

I like to remember this passage from Freeman Dyson's *Imagined Worlds*: "Ten years is, as Shakespeare knew, the normal horizon of human activities, the time we take to educate a child, to launch a career, to establish a business. . . . Ten years is also the outer limit of political predictability. In ten years, governments change, political leaders rise and fall, empires collapse, wars and revolutions turn the world upside down."

The message? In thinking, the time frame doesn't have to be today's juiced-up schedule of deliver it yesterday. Often, the best ideas take time and, sometimes, the horizon of Shakespeare's time should be the horizon today.

PEOPLE WHO DON'T BELIEVE IN GOD DON'T HAVE A PRAYER

And then there's **prayer**. I'm not the type to

wear my faith on my sleeve, but I do know — and am not ashamed to say — that the best ideas I have are sudden spiritual feelings. I call them epiphanies. They arrive when I visualize the ideas coming through me rather than out of me. As a motivational speaker, I've addressed more than half a million people around the world. Just because I speak a lot doesn't mean I don't get nervous. As a matter of fact, a year ago I started getting pretty bad jitters before speaking.

I made an appointment with the famed psychologist, Arthur Cohen. He suggested that I just let the light through, that is, become a vessel. The next speech I gave was my best, and to this day I don't speak. I just let the light through.

Puccini, who wrote the music of *Madame Butterfly*, claims it was dictated to him by God. Morant said he wasn't sure where his ideas came from; he could only state, "I pray to God and the composition comes." William Blake tells us that the poem "Milton" was "dictated and the authors are in eternity." Ralph Waldo Emerson wrote, "The poet sometimes seems to have a chamber in his brain into which an angel flies with divine messages." Cicero claimed, "No one was ever great without divine inspiration." And Rudyard Kipling warned, "I have learned that when your inner helper is in charge, do not try to think consciously. Drift — wait — and obey." The great artist Mark Rothko says, "The people who weep before my pictures are having the same religious experience I had when I painted them." And finally, Blake adds that the one power that makes a poet is divine vision.

The bottom line is that the biggest idea in the

world is and always will be God. I believe that many of my best ideas are as much spiritual *Ahas!* as intellectual ones. In trying to think in concert with the most creative force in the world — whoever your God is — my wife and I brainstormed on an idea for a new kind of spa. When we had a good germ of an idea, we did two things. First, we put ourselves in the place of our future guests. Second, we asked to be creatively guided by greater sources than ourselves. Out of this ideation came our best idea.

LITTLE HORSE:
THE SPA FOR THE SPIRIT

Nestled in the North Georgia mountains on 215 acres of land will rise a spa for not only the body but also for the mind and spirit.

Its unique centerpiece will be the Discovery P.A.T.H, an acronym for "People Achieving True Happiness." On the two-mile circular path, guests will have light psychological experiences that alter their thinking. One example of this is the Forgiving Phone. You will find it about five-hundred yards down the path; a white phone. A sign will read:

> *As a guest of Little Horse, you are welcome to call anyone you wish, anywhere in the world, and speak as long as you would like. Provided you are calling to forgive the person.*

Other experiences include a perpetual rainbow and the SymphonTree™ — thirty-six trees that emanate the sounds of instruments in an orchestra. As you walk amongst the trees, your ears are filled with blossoms of music.

These experiences are provided to guests to enhance the way they think. Ultimately they will leave Little Horse with a new peace of mind, or perhaps I should spell it "piece." Little Horse will be an amusement park for the spirit. We plan to open in the year 2001.

I've had a lot of ideas over the years, but all of them in various ways blended **passion, persistence, percolation,** and **prayer.** I wrote a ballet called *Jump*, based on the notion that you have to meet a lot of princes before you find your frog. The story revolves around a beautiful princess who suffers an identity crisis when she learns that all the frogs in the land of Miltonrose want to kiss her to obtain princehood. Later she kisses a frog and turns into one herself. The two hop off happily ever after. Some ideas take longer than others. This one has percolated for twenty years, but it appears that it may be performed next year in New York City.

Some of my favorite ideas have just been goofy. In college, I received an A-plus in journalism for writing a parody of *Playboy* called *Playgoy* . . . the magazine for Jews posing as Christians. The one ad that is most characteristic of my career is a photograph of Mikhail Gorbachev smiling and waving above the prominently painted slogan, "It's my party and I'll do what I want to." In smaller type beneath this, "Citizens for Glasnost congratulate Gorbachev for his efforts to help unite the world powers." I have two reasons why it's my favorite: first, it makes you smile, and second, I created the ad from scratch, as well as the organization. Like wind without a sail, I had a great idea without a client, so I created that, too.

The one ad most characteristic of brainstorming was the Young and Tender Chicken TV commercial. The client wanted to drive home the brand-name. The idea we brainstormed was to take a dozen eleven-month-old babies and make them dance to the funky chicken. Nothing is more young and tender than adorable babies. The result was the first digital commercial of its kind shot by Kevin Dole. It won all sorts of awards, including one at the Cannes Film Festival.

Brainstorming several years ago about how to get Hawaiian Tropic some free press, we recommended that the company send suntan lotion to Norman Schwartzkopf and the "Desert Storm" troops so that they could "save face." I convinced Cadillac to position themselves against Japanese cars and created a TV spot where Kamikaze pilots were shot down. That commercial caused such a stir that it led the six o'clock news. By 7 P.M. no one would ever see it again. The good news is that Cadillac captured lots of new customers. For Del Monte, I illustrated their logo as big as possible on a poster without the words Del Monte. Below the illustration were the words, "Take this eye test. If you don't see the words Del Monte above, you have not been eating your fruits and vegetables." The Bahamas Ministry of Tourism handed me their $30 million account after I convinced them that it was "Hip to Hop to the Bahamas." There are more than seven hundred islands, but most Americans go only to Nassau. That simple expression started people thinking of alternatives. The idea we had for GTE cellular phones was to tell people that they finally had a carrier whose signal was clear. Remember when they used to break up? In this campaign, we had Neil Sedaka re-record "Breaking Up is Hard to Do" for GTE.

When Coca-Cola was having problems selling to teens in malls, I came up with the concept of Icebreakers™. Here's the idea. The late Coke patriarch and chairman Robert Woodruff vowed to put Coca-Cola within arm's reach of everyone. He saw Coke as a social facilitator that would bring people together. Back then, kids shared a Coke at a soda fountain with their date. How could we recreate that experience for today's cynical teens? My idea was to set up a Coca-Cola kiosk at shopping malls. Teens could get a Coke and be asked questions such as, "What's more important: money or love? What would you rather do on a Saturday night: watch a movie with your date or go dancing? What kind of music do you like: country and western or rock?" A Coca-Cola attendant would key in the responses the way a McDonald's attendant

---

Oldest Idea

ARISTOTLE ACTUALLY WAS THINKING FOR A LIVING BEFORE ANYONE ELSE, AND IT PAID OFF. WHILE THINKING HE INVENTED THE STUDY OF LOGIC AND APPLIED ITS PRINCIPLES TO PHYSICS, CHEMISTRY, BIOLOGY, AND ZOOLOGY. WHAT'S MORE, AS A PHILOSOPHER AND WRITER HE SET THE STANDARD FOR WESTERN THINKING.

would key in Happy Meal orders. Then the teenager would get a 1½-by-1½ inch plastic ice cube with the Coca-Cola logo spinning inside it. Buried in each of the Icebreakers™ would be not only vital information about the teen, but also a music chip. When an Icebreaker™ got within ten feet of another Icebreaker™ coded with similar preferences and owned by a member of the opposite sex, suddenly the teens would hear the first ten musical notes of the "Always Coca-Cola" jingle. Coke, in the end, held off on doing the campaign. But don't be surprised if you see a similar version being used by another company before too long.

And then there was my take on the idea of the century.

HOW I SOLVED THE PROBLEM OF THE CENTURY

"No problem can stand the assault of sustained thinking," said Voltaire, and this would be proof. The millennium is approaching and Prime Minister Tony Blair of Great Britain is in need of a big idea.

His Labour Party, upon being elected for the first time in years, inherited the Millennium Project — 181 acres on the North Greenwich Peninsula on the River Thames. Upon it will be built Millennium Village. Its centerpiece will be a dome, twice the size of the Georgia Dome in Atlanta, which is currently the largest building of its type in the world. What will be the idea that captures the attention of the world at the stroke of midnight on January 1, 2000? And will this idea sustain perhaps the largest New Year's Eve celebration in the world?

The technique of thinking I used to answer these questions was role playing. I played the role of Tony Blair. After all, I — the Prime Minister, that is — had a great deal on the line. Whatever idea I create I must then raise money to support, so it better be one that multinational corporations can get behind. Still, it must capture the hearts of the British, the Scottish, the Irish, and the Welsh. It must be about the future of the United Kingdom, not just its past.

I have often found the best ideas where you would least expect them — sitting right next to the problem. And that's where I found H. G. Wells. Greenwich is where time started. It's where it will start in the year 2000. (Actually, it will begin on an island near China, but the official clock is in Greenwich.) And thirteen miles from the Millennium Dome is where the father of time travel was born. Bingo!

My big idea was the H. G. Wells Time Machine Millennium Experience. It would be based on Wells's *Time Machine*, one of eighty novels the visionary and early founder of the Labour Party wrote. The Millennium Experience would be the continuation of that journey, an attempt to out-Disney Disney that would take visitors in time-mobiles to destinations at far-flung points in history.

Families could meet Monet while he was painting water lilies, take part in the Renaissance of Italy, visit with the framers of the U.S. Constitution, ride into the American Wild West. They could go to an early Beatles concert in Hamburg, Germany, witness the coronation of Queen Victoria in 1840, buy a ticket to Mars, and eat lunch with dinosaurs.

Sponsors would jump at a chance to create a meaningful experience for their consumers. Microsoft could actually take people to *where they want to go — today!* Swatch could promise you *the time of the century.* Kodak could take you *further.* Century 21 could take visitors on a ride through all 21 centuries, and Coca-Cola could be there, *always.*

Not all my ideas have been brain surgery, and I'll be the first to admit that some may be doomed to live on as great ideas that will never become reality. Some of them probably should live on as great ideas rather than become reality. But I'd like to think that what they share is a sense of adventure, of fun, of the promise of bright thinking painted outside the lines.

If you manage to instill that sense of adventure, fun, and promise in your thinking, you're going to instill it in your life as well. You have to remember always that none of us just thinks. Thinking is everything. It is the most important

---

THE IDEA THAT CHANGED MUSIC

BORN ROBERT ZIMMERMAN IN 1941, BOBBY WAS CONSIDERED AN INCREDIBLY CREATIVE POET. HE TAUGHT HIMSELF THE PIANO, GUITAR, AND HARMONICA. INSPIRED BY THE POET DYLAN THOMAS, THIS JEWISH KID FROM DULUTH, MINNESOTA, CHANGED HIS NAME TO BOB DYLAN. HE IS KNOWN FOR FUSING FOLK & ROCK, THEN MERGING COUNTRY AND WESTERN WITH FUNK & ROCK AND LATER EXPLORING LATINO, SOUL, AND CARIBBEAN MUSIC. HIS IDEAS WOULD TAKE MUSIC TO PLACES NEVER HEARD BEFORE.

act of our lives. We do it every day, and when we do it, it affects everyone. It's as valuable as breathing. Air keeps us alive, but thinking creates our lives. How we think affects our health, impacts our wealth, and most importantly gives meaning to why we are here.

So if we really went in that time machine, the one insight that should hit us over the head time and again is that thinking is our most valuable asset. From the past it teaches us. In the present it motivates us. And in the future it steers each of us to a unique destiny. I can't tell you what your destiny is. But I can tell you that shaping the one you want is within your grasp, just as I was able to get my thumb up and think my way to a recovery in that hospital room in Italy. All it takes is the **passion, persistence, percolation,** and **prayer** to make it happen.

CHAPTER 6

S.O.S., Slinky, and You: Thinking Your Way to a Smarter Career

"I thought about it all the time."
— Sir Isaac Newton on how
he discovered the law of gravity

CONSIDER THE SLINKY. Sinuous, silly, simple. It was a great toy when you were a kid, it's a great toy for your kids, and it will be a great toy for your kids' kids.

Did you ever wonder how the Slinky came to be?

It all started with a mechanical engineer named Richard James. He was working during World War II to test the horsepower of battleships, using a measuring device called a torsion meter. One day one of these meters fell on the floor and rolled toward him. He thought of children, then his thoughts jumped back to his metal wire meter. This would make a great toy, he surmised. His wife, Betty, began the search for a name, when she came across the item's definition in the dictionary, "sleek and sinuous in movement." The Slinky was born. By the 1950s, Betty and her thinking-for-a-living husband had six children and an incredible business built around one product. Unfortunately, her husband had another idea — to join a religious cult in Bolivia.

Betty James stayed and built the company into a cult itself. Today, James' Industries generates more than $15 million in revenue annually.

Slinkies have been used in pecan picking, as a pigeon repellent, and as drapery tiebacks. During the Vietnam War Slinkies were used as makeshift radio antennas. A Slinky is on display at the Smithsonian Institute, the Metropolitan Museum of Art, and my sons' playroom. Not bad for a single offbeat idea.

Then consider the S.O.S. soap pad. Back in 1912, an enterprising gentleman named Edwin Cox was selling Wear-Ever aluminum cookware door-to-door. It was a good business, but it had one major problem. Customers complained that aluminum pots were too hard to clean. Cox thought if he could solve the cleaning problem, he could financially clean up. He began experimenting at home and soon hit upon the magic combination. He made steel balls and packed them with soap. His wife suggested a name for his new kitchen helper: Save Our Saucepans. When abbreviated, it became known as S.O.S. Today Americans use two million every day.

Slinking around or cleaning up, these are great examples of the fine art of thinking for a living — two unconventional little ideas that turned idiosyncratic sparks of creativity into fortunes. So the question isn't whether you can think for a living. These days you have to. The question is how best to do it. I think you do it in four main ways: (1) by choosing your proper domain, (2) by slowing down, (3) by learning to protect your ideas, and (4) by learning to line jump or think creatively outside the lines.

How to Be a Thinker

This is the golden age of thinking for a living, whether you do it on your own or at a company where ideas are rewarded and nurtured. The consulting industry is now estimated to be worth $50 billion worldwide. The big consulting companies charge as much as $750,000 per project. McKinsey & Company, Bain & Company, Andersen Consulting, Gemini Consulting, Boston Consulting Group, and my company, BrightHouse, have seen some of the largest thinking contacts in the world. Their missions are to review and restructure companies in hopes of providing value to the companies' bottom lines. Regardless of methodology, all these companies think for a living.

IDEA FOR PEACE

IN HIS QUEST FOR TRUTH, MORALITY, AND SPIRITUAL RENEWAL, MAHATMA GANDHI SHOWED MILLIONS THE ROAD TO PEACE. CONSIDERED TO BE THE FATHER OF INDIA, GANDHI INSPIRED MAJOR POLICY CHANGE THROUGH NON-VIOLENCE. IMAGINE CHANGING THE WORLD'S MIND WITHOUT PUTTING A GUN TO ITS HEAD.

Independent businessmen and businesswomen also are thinking for a living. For example, financial planners and attorneys think on behalf of their clients. I employ such a firm to think about my family's financial future and well-being. Psychologists and psychiatrists think on behalf of our thinking.

There was a time not long ago when most people made a living through brawn, not brains, and most companies succeeded by getting there first and working harder. Today that's not good enough. You can't get to the twenty-first century on cruise control. Doing one thing over and over won't cut it. But if that's a sobering thought, it's also an empowering one because the flip side is that the ideation era about to dawn will be the most democratic in history.

Gloria Bromell-Tinubu, an economist at Spelman College — the prestigious, historically black women's college in Atlanta that's rated as one of the best liberal arts colleges in the country — sees astonishing opportunities in a world where ideas are the real capital. Moving toward a world where ideas matter more than inherited wealth or IQ or social class, she said, will open up the economy like nothing before. "We broaden and expand the capacity of capitalism," she said. "We transform capitalism, in fact, into a more egalitarian kind of social or economic system. Because for the first time, then, we really have equal access."

This process is already well underway. A Brookings Institution study has found that 75 percent of the productivity in the U.S. economy can be attributed to education and knowledge. And most businesses have long since learned —

at least in the abstract — that their futures depend on constantly reenergizing their idea base. "Companies spend more money today on equipment that gathers, processes, analyzes, and distributes information than on machines that stamp, cut, assemble, lift, and otherwise manipulate the physical world," says *Fortune Magazine* editor Thomas Stewart and author of *Intellectual Capital*.

Says Fumio Kodama, a professor of innovation policy at Satima University near Tokyo, "If R&D investment begins to surpass capital investment, the corporation could be said to be shifting from being a place of production to being a place for thinking. More and more, thinking has become more valuable. Resumes now list big ideas. After all, who cares about where you went to school? It's not where, but what you did with your education."

So how can you make this work for you?

The first rule to remember is that thinkers come in all sizes and shapes. You don't have to be McKinsey, a lawyer, or a psychologist to be a thinker. Once a carpenter was a guy who sawed boards and hammered nails. Today there are carpenters who are artists, guys who can visualize what kind of piece is needed, whether it should be ash, cedar, or pine, how to paint it, and how to design it. They're not consultants in Hermes ties and Brooks Brothers suits, but, if they're good, they think for a living. There are little flashes of creativity in whatever you do — the way you cut hair, sell real estate, paint, design landscapes — that are forms of thinking for a living.

So here's the thing you must keep in mind at

all times — the world isn't divided into thinkers and drones, creative types with fancy jobs who think for a living and worker bees plodding along in search of a paycheck. Whatever you do, think of it as an art, as a canvas, as a tapestry in which you can apply your best ideas and special talents.

If we remember what Csikzentmihalyi said about domain — the arena in which creativity plays out — the first key to plotting your career has to be **finding the right environment, the right domain for your talents.** I never intended to be an adman, but, in fact, it was where I belonged, where my creative instincts were given the most room to run. Indeed, the first requirement of genius is finding the right environment for your talents to play out.

Consider, the case of Charles Darwin, a man whose ideas forever changed our view of human evolution. But in the year of the publication of his work *On the Origin of Species* Darwin wrote: "I suppose I am a very slow thinker." His son Francis said that his father "used to say of himself that he was not quick enough to hold an argument with anyone, and I think this was true." Given all that, what better place for Darwin's intelligence to focus on than the long, slow, mysterious march of human evolution? In today's Darwinian business environment, Darwin himself had the first rule down cold: Find the right domain, so your talents can reach their full potential.

For many of us this can be a long process of trial and error. Michael Jordan may have loved the sultry pace of baseball, but his proper domain is clearly basketball. Say what you like about Bill Clinton, but if ever a man was born to be a politician, he's that man. There's nothing so joyous as watching a true artist create and nothing so deadening as watching someone living out someone else's dream — the free spirit stuck in the family law firm, the surgeon who wants to be a sculptor, the adman who dreams about writing fiction. I'm not saying that everyone gets to live their ideal life. But I am saying that if you want to unleash your creativity, to think for a living in a way that gets you excited every morning about going to work, you first have to check your gut and ask yourself what you really want to do, where your creativity feels truly at home, and then figure out a way to do it.

Rule No. 2 is **slow down**. No one does their best thinking on fast forward. Years ago, there was an advertising public service campaign against cocaine and other drugs such as amphetamines. The headline emblazoned across our media was "Speed Kills." That's still relevant. Speed kills great ideas. The faster we speed up, the less time we have to think, to incubate, to ponder, to dream. The "faster than a speeding bullet" philosophy is really apparent in the advertising world. Today when the marketing writers and art directors are given an assignment, they're also given very little time. Their salaries are lucrative, their offices are spacious, but their ideas are getting smaller and smaller because the time they have to incubate is decreasing. All our energies are focused on creating relationships as opposed to creating *within* a relationship.

THE TITANIC
EFFECT

Through the tragic story of the Titanic, we learn that the probable reason for hitting the iceberg was the fact that the owner of the shipping line, Whitestar, wanted to reach New York's harbor ahead of schedule. So he ordered the captain to speed up. Consequently, the ship could not slow down to maneuver its way out of danger once the crew spotted the iceberg. This is what happens to ideas without incubation. In condensing the time that we have to think, we also shorten the probability of success. I have created hundreds of advertising campaigns for clients, and I can tell you in hindsight that over the last twenty-two years, the strategies I thought about and the ideas that I pondered worked for those clients. On the other hand, the schemes that I put together under duress or under pressure or on a deadline were not as successful.

The magazine *Fast Company* now clocks the average business lunch at thirty-six minutes. Environmental activist Jeremy Rifkin was one of the first to raise questions about the desirability of speed in his 1987 book *Time Wars.* "We have quickened the pace of life only to become less patient," he wrote. "We have become more organized, but less spontaneous, less joyful. We are better prepared to act on the future, but less able to enjoy the present and reflect on the past."

COUNTING TIME IS
NOT SO IMPORTANT AS
MAKING TIME COUNT

Woody Allen once said he took a speed-reading course and read *War and Peace* in twenty minutes. "It involves Russia," he quipped. Too many of us read, write, and have relationships at that speed. And at breakneck speed, one is bound to have an accident. And yet we continue to try to find ways to make things faster. Distance is no longer a serious obstacle to modern travel, but time remains unconquerable. Perhaps that's why we are so obsessed with it. For time cannot be expanded, accumulated, mortgaged . . . it's the one thing that's beyond our control.

People have been trying to create more time for centuries. First they realized that donkeys were faster than walking; then that horses were faster than donkeys; that steam engines were faster than sails. Then something really incredible happened — the invention of the telephone. That was followed by windup clocks and bicycles. By the turn of the century, the leisurely three-quarter time of the waltz was on the way out, as Scott Joplin ushered in his bouncy, ragtime classic "Maple Leaf Rag." That, of course, gave way to jazz, boogie woogie, rock 'n' roll, disco, and finally techno, which races along at about two hundred beats per minute.

In 1913 Henry Ford introduced the assembly line, cutting the time required to produce a car from fourteen person hours to just two. The Roaring Twenties were just that. In 1937 Dale Carnegie's book *How to Win Friends and*

Influence People became a big hit. Some believe it was a success because it showed people how to make friends in a hurry. In 1953 Carl Swanson introduced the first TV dinner.

A 1960 study proved that there had been a drop in household chores but driving, shopping, and longer hours at work were filling up the extra time. And then in 1971 Madison Avenue realized that TV ads could be made in half the time. So they went from a sixty-second format to a thirty-second format. By the 1980s they would be at a fifteen-second format.

In 1973 Federal Express made thinking much faster. Or at least took the thinking, put it in bags, and got it to people much faster. And in 1980 the nanosecond was born, a measure of time lasting one billionth of a second. By the 1980s Federal Express almost seemed tortoise-like compared to fax machines. Also, in the 1980s cellular phones hit. And then, of course, E-mail.

THE INCUBATION NATION

So it's clear that we can always find ways to do it faster. The trick is to find ways to do it better and smarter. If we are to think better, think more

---

BIGGER THAN A DINOSAUR IDEA

HE WORE A PLAID SHIRT, BLUE JEANS, AND COWBOY BOOTS. HE HAD FORTY-EIGHT FRECKLES — ONE FOR EACH STATE OF THE UNION AT THE TIME. IN 1948, HE RAN FOR PRESIDENT AND RECEIVED MORE THAN A MILLION VOTES. FIVE YEARS LATER, HE HAD A DAILY TV AUDIENCE TOTALING MORE VIEWERS THAN BARNEY CURRENTLY ATTRACTS WEEKLY. SAY HI TO HOWDY DOODY, THE FIRST CHILDREN'S TV STAR.

creatively, be more original, we will need more time to think. If you want to accelerate your thinking, you must slow down. When you slow down, you become mindful. Henry David Thoreau's two years at Walden Pond were, above all, a mindful experience. Thoreau wrote, "Time is but the stream I go a fishing in. I drink in it. But while I drink, I see the sandy bottom and detect how shallow it is. Its thin current slides away, but eternity remains. I would drink deeper, fish in the sky whose bottom is pebbly with stars."

Mindfulness has been called the heart of Buddhist meditation. Frankly, it's a simple concept. Jon Kabat-Zinn, in his book *Wherever You Go, There You Are*, says, "Mindfulness means paying attention in a particular way. On purpose, in the present moment, and nonjudgmentally."

Rule No. 3 will become more and more important as the next century unfolds. Indeed, it's one of the quiet battlegrounds of our economic system right now. Do you know how to make sure you get paid for your ideas? Can you guarantee that your intellectual property is as well protected as your physical property? If the answer is no — and it probably is — you need to start thinking more about the value of your thinking. History is littered with people who came up with great ideas and saw others profit from them. You need to make sure you don't join their ranks.

PROTECT YOUR BRAIN

One of my dear friends is a brilliant trademark attorney. When I asked him about protecting your brain, he suggested the following. First, you must protect your ideas as soon as you come up with them. Depending upon the type and form of the idea, any one of a number of different bodies of law comes into play including patent, trademarks, copyright, and trade secret law. All of these methods of protecting ideas are different in scope and application, and it is best to consult with your lawyer early in the ideation process so that you obtain as much protection as possible.

Even before consulting a lawyer, however, there are some things you can do to protect your idea. First, in order to establish your ownership of the concept, it is best to write it down in detail and to date the writing. Then mail a copy of the idea to yourself in a sealed envelope which you do not open.

CAN YOU KEEP A SECRET?

Keep the idea secret. Do not, in a spurt of enthusiasm, tell all your friends about the idea. If you need to discuss it with someone, make it clear, preferably in writing, that the person to whom you disclose the idea should keep the information strictly confidential. If you work with others in developing ideas, you should have written agreements with those individuals determining who owns the ideas you come up with.

Obviously, if you want to exploit the idea commercially, it is best to disclose it in confidence to potential business partners or prospective customers. A simple idea submission letter requiring the recipient to agree to keep the concept confidential, unless he or she decides to pay for it, is always advisable, although some companies refuse to sign such letters.

Now, for the law.

Patents protect ideas that have been reduced to practice, that is, embodied in an invention. Such ideas must be useful, novel, and nonobvious. The typical "utility" patent covers an apparatus or article of manufacture, a process or method or a composition of matter, and lasts for at least seventeen years from the date of the issuance of a patent. Design patent protection is directed to the physical appearance of the item that is patented. A patent is valuable because it gives its owner the ability to exclude others from making, using, selling, offering for sale, or importing whatever is claimed in the patent.

A patent is, however, often difficult and expensive to obtain and, depending upon the patent's scope, may be easy to circumvent. Also, it often takes several years to patent an item, which makes patents less valuable for ideas that, by their very nature, need to be exploited quickly and have a short "shelf life." Finally, pure ideas, which have not been reduced "to practice" do not qualify for patent protection.

Even if patent protection is not available for your idea, do not despair. Many people have made a great deal of money selling nonpatentable items, and the records of the U.S. Patent Office are full of patents that are not worth a dime. Besides, there are other methods of protection.

MARK THIS IDEA DOWN

If part of your idea involves the use of a distinctive name or logo, then you should consider obtaining a federal trademark or service mark registration for that name or logo.

The more original and less descriptive the name or logo, the stronger the mark will be. Even before registration, whenever the name or logo is used, you should include the notices ™(for trademark) or ᔆᴹ(for service mark) next to your proposed mark. This will put others on notice that you consider that mark to be your property. By "tying down" the name of the product or service, you will have a leg up on those who may attempt to exploit your idea once it is disclosed.

Copyright law protects the expression of an idea, not the idea itself. For example, a book about a system of accounting is subject to copyright, but the copyright does not protect the idea or ideas used in the actual system of accounting itself. If your idea involves a number of visual and/or artistic elements, however, copyright law will protect these distinctive "expressions" of your idea. Also, copyright merely prevents the copying of your work. It does not prevent others from independently creating other similar works, as long as copying is not involved.

Unlike some other forms of protection, where you have to take certain steps to obtain protection, one's rights as a copyright owner vest initially at the moment the work (the writing, book, CD-ROM, computer program, etc.) is created. You will not forfeit any truly valuable protection by failing to register your work immediately. Even so, though the law no longer requires it, it is best to include a copyright notice on the work in a conspicuous place. A proper notice should contain the word "copyright" or an abbreviated version of it, the year of creation of the work, and the name of the author, for example: "© 1998 BrightHouse, LLP." Such a notice will, at the least, deter someone from the outright copying of the work that contains your idea.

FOR YOUR EYES ONLY

Like patent protection, trade secret protection guards ideas. Such ideas must not be generally known, must be subject to reasonable efforts to guard their secrecy, and should be, as a result, valuable. In order to maintain the ability to claim trade secrecy, however, you must take steps to limit the disclosure of the secret idea only to persons who have a "need to know" the idea. This involves at a minimum the use of confidentiality and nondisclosure agreements and other security measures. It is a good idea to mark any documents containing the idea as CONFIDENTIAL, PROPRIETARY, OR TRADE SECRET. Keep in mind that trade secret protection is most worthwhile when you are preparing to exploit an idea. Once the idea becomes public, however, the secrecy of the idea evaporates, and you will need to turn to other methods of protection.

For more information about protecting your ideas, call 1-800-PTO-9199; that's the Patent and Trademark Office.

LINE JUMPING

Here's Rule No. 4 for a thinking career. Learn how to jump and do it every time you approach a creative challenge. I'm not talking about literally jumping (though I'll get to that a little later). I'm talking about line jumping, a quality of mind in which the unexpected, the offbeat, and the unconventional insights become the rule.

In marketing, we have an expression called line extension. If you have a strong brand, the theory goes, you can create another using the appeal of the former brand. Diet Coke is a brand that borrowed the goodwill of the name Coca-Cola. Subsequently it became successful on its own. Reese's Peanut Butter Cups gave birth to Reese's Peanut Butter. Just open your pantry and you'll see line extensions all over the place. These are all examples of extensional thinking. Your mind says A, which leads to B, and then to C.

In line jumping, by comparison, A leads to L or Q or Z. Here's an example I thought of during the recent assault on cigarette companies. Though I personally would not work on behalf of a cigarette manufacturer, the Marlboro Man has always intrigued me. When I smoked (I gave it up in 1987), I was a Marlboro Man. When I lit up, it took me out West. Even now, when I hear the Marlboro theme song "The Magnificent Seven," it makes me want to saddle up and ride over to the convenience store for a smoke.

So what is Marlboro to do, now that new advertising restrictions prohibit TV, radio, and now pictures of the product? Banning all advertising is right around the corner. The answer is line jump.

That is, open hotels. Imagine the Marlboro Dude Ranch where you can be a real Marlboro Man. You wouldn't have to show a pack of cigarettes anywhere. The only hint of the pack itself would be the red roof of the ranch house, which from a distance would look like the top of the Marlboro box.

This is a line jump, or an example of nonlinear thinking.

As thinkers, line jumping can be an enormous amount of fun. It's great exercise for your brain, and you just might create the next big thing.

As citizens living in a nonlinear world, we need to think in a nonlinear fashion because change is nonlinear.

In the *Age of Unreason*, Charles Handy describes the age of change in which we live. "Change used to be more of the same, only better, but not anymore. Today, change is discontinuity."

Jean-Marie Dru, in his book *Disruption*, elaborates. "Change no longer follows a pattern. That is why we must start thinking upside down, backward and forward, and inside and out." He says that many companies encourage what he calls "a culture of incrementalism. That is, a little improvement here, a little line extension there." These are all baby steps. What's needed are giant steps. "For companies, success lies in questioning and mobility. Companies must create new worlds. They must constantly do, undo, and redo. To accomplish this they must adopt a mindset of anticipation. They can no longer surf the wave; instead they must

---

A SHARP IDEA

"IF I HAD BEEN TECHNICALLY TRAINED, I WOULD HAVE QUIT," SAID KING GILLETTE AFTER SPENDING EIGHT YEARS INVENTING AND INTRODUCING HIS SAFETY RAZOR.

become the wind that creates the wave."

Management guru Tom Peters says, "Don't rock the boat. Sink it and start over." Creative destruction is fundamental to all change. The new can only be created by destroying the old. As Picasso said, "The painter must destroy. He must destroy to give it another life." Frank Lloyd Wright was so destructive that the *New York Times* called him "the anarchist of architecture." Anyone afraid of destroying the old to get to the new never will be able to achieve a worthwhile, breakthrough innovation.

Many companies hire an ideation firm because their own corporate culture works against unique thinking. The culture says, "Don't think outside the square, or you may find yourself outside the company." This is the kind of culture that rewards stodgy thinking and dull, safe ideas. At the same time, it strangles great thinking.

Companies and environments that have a "certain" way of doing things — that are stuck in a rut of routine thinking — will undo any possibility of having breakthrough ideas.

ROUTINIZATION RUINS INNOVATION

Beware of people and companies that "do it by the book." Bastions of procedure create idea anorexia — thoughts that think they are big but are really small.

Do you know what happens to people who get into a groove? The groove becomes a rut, and the rut becomes a grave.

Roger von Oech, author of *A Whack on the*

Side of the Head, encourages us to "slay our sacred cows" — rules that limit our thoughts and actions. "Try some exercises in what-iffing." What if you could succeed at anything in the world? What would it be? What if you were hired by President Clinton to clean up the environment? What would you invent? What if the world were made of chocolate? Roald Dahl, the creator of *Willy Wonka's Chocolate Factory*, turned his iffing into a living.

Another one of Roger von Oech's incredibly helpful insights is, "When everyone thinks alike, no one is doing much thinking." Von Oech points out that in the olden days, a king would hire a jester. Unlike the king's "yes men," the fool would often shed light on a truth. Parody, irreverence, disruption, metaphors, and analogies were the tools of the jester's trade. The same instruments are used to create ideas. So think like a fool. Make fun of the status quo. Be irreverent with the original. Disrupt convention. The old Italian saying applies: *Impara l'arte, e mettila da parte* (Learn the craft, and then set it aside). Philosophize with yourself. Reverse your point of view. Then reverse it again. Take risks. The only risk in your career is not taking a risk with your career.

A lot of people think line jumpers are born, not made. They're wrong. I know I've always had a talent for unconventional thoughts, but I also know I've studied creativity relentlessly and that any number of writers have put together their own road maps for thinking outside the lines. In his book, *Escape from the Maze*, James Higgins, a professor of management at Rollins College in Winter Park, Florida, says the biggest obstacle to creativity may be that we think we can't "cheat" — we think there's a single way to approach every problem. In fact, the way out of the maze may be digging a tunnel or pole-vaulting out, rather than endlessly traversing the corridors looking for the open door at the end. Higgins's book is about training ourselves to be line jumpers. He suggest nine steps toward personal creativity. A few examples:

Unlearn how not to be creative — Start breaking the habits of predictable thinking you grew up with and probably still instinctively use.

Use creativity techniques — Such as brainstorming, mind-mapping, and storyboarding to learn new and more creative ways to think.

Learn when to think — There are times, just before bed or in the middle of vigorous exercise, for example, when the mind's censors are turned off and the line jumps are more likely to come.

Reach out to the right brain — Especially if you're a (logical and orderly) left-brain person. That could mean forcing yourself to think in pictures rather than words.

THE CREATIVE MIND IS OPEN TWENTY-FOUR HOURS A DAY

A career in thinking is tough. Henry Ford said, "Thinking is the hardest work there is, which is probably why so few engage in it."

When I tell people I am a thinker, they usually have two responses. The first is complete shock and disbelief. "Wow, what's a thinker? How do you do that?" The other one is "What do you think about?" The answers are similar.

A thinker thinks about everything.

As a thinker, you need to read, write, and experience. Do things you've never done. Do things you did as a child. Buy a dollhouse and a train set. Take the day off and go to the zoo. Meditate. Take a yoga class. Take any class. Create time for yourself where you can incubate; your mind needs this space. Once again, Csikszentmihalyi offers great insight into what he calls "the mysterious time when the process of creativity usually goes underground for a while." He says, "Incubation has often been thought of as the most creative part of the process."

Scientist and author Freeman Dyson describes his current work this way: "I am fooling around not doing anything, which probably means that this is a creative period, although of course you don't know until afterward."

I think it is very important to be idle. People who keep themselves busy all the time are generally not creative, so I am not ashamed of being idle.

As Tom Peters, author of *Liberation Management* and *In Search of Excellence* writes in his *Tom Peters Seminar*, "The race will go to the curious, the slightly mad, and those with an unsatiated passion for learning and daredeviltry." This is the same man who rightly claims that the "only factory asset is the human imagination." It's a nice thought — that the race can go to the passionate and the slightly unhinged, rather than to the cold, gray line of those who follow every rule. It's also true. I've bet my career on it. You can too.

THIS JUST IN

One more thought about how to think about your career: Should you choose to become a thinker, you will find that your goals will change. Thinkers don't climb ladders nor are thinkers part of the rat race. Unlike rodents trying to get out of a maze, to get to the cheese, thinkers enjoy what's around them. After all, what's around you is a lot to think about.

In 1997, my wife, Cynthia, was bringing home a big salary. She had worked her way up to the prestigious chair of the lead anchor for WAGA-TV in Atlanta, the number one Fox station in the country.

The news business is murder, literally. Local newscast reports are filled with the atrocities of life. Against this grim backdrop, our beautiful son Julien was born two years ago. Along with his older brother, Alden, a miniature horse, and two cats, we were a full-fledged family.

After an enormous amount of thought, Cynthia decided to ask the then news director for two mornings off to spend with her children. The guy looked at the ground, and his face turned red. Her request wasn't much to ask for, but it was too much for him.

Rather than subject herself to an old company way of thinking, Cynthia had to think for herself. She left that high-profile job for something much greater. She chose family and flexibility over the corporate gray line. What she didn't anticipate was the bonus she would receive along the way.

Today, Cynthia is thinking for a living. She has

published several books. A different TV station is producing her own creation, "Good For Parents," a unique parenting show headed for national syndication. What's more, Alden and Julien got five mornings instead of two with their mother, and Cynthia became her own boss. As for her six-figure salary, she's now making twice as much. The story here is good news for thinkers.

THE AGE OF THE FAMILLIONAIRE

A career as a thinker takes more than putting suggestions in a box. It means thinking about yourself — the only one of you in the universe — and the people around you. In the 1980s it was fashionable to put the family aside for the greater good of the family. Accumulate more for their benefit. But this was a myth of the highest order. Families who put financial success ahead of emotional success get shortchanged.

Worse yet, people who don't live their own life will die having never truly lived. Cynthia hopefully will live a long life, but by following her own line of thought, she is already living a wider life. She is a famillionaire — a person who found her fortune in her family by being true to herself.

Author Joan Peters has written a thought-provoking book, *When Mothers Work*. She says

---

DID THIS THINKER HAVE ANY IDEA?

IT'S IRONIC THAT THE MAN WHO SCULPTED "THE THINKER" NEVER PROFITED FINANCIALLY FROM HIS MASTERPIECES. RODIN LEFT ALL OF HIS WORKS TO HIS COUNTRY.

that 50 percent of marriages end in divorce when couples do not balance their lives at home with the demands of work. The good news is that famillionaires are popping up all over, like the forty-nine-year-old president of American Express, who gave up his prestigious job to spend 40 percent more time with his children. He says he feels "as productive and content as ever. The conflict is gone." This is the thinking of a famillionaire and a happy family.

Like a functional family that creates a positive environment for its members, companies are beginning to do the same. Therefore, as a thinker you must follow your train of thought rather than train to be someone you're not. In the end, the biggest thought about your career has to be what it is and what it is not. It may be your livelihood, but your family is your life. If you're smart, you'll never forget the distinction.

CHAPTER 7

CREATING A THINKING COMPANY

You can't use up creativity.
The more you use, the more you have.
Sadly, too often creativity is
smothered rather than nurtured.
There has to be a climate in which
new ways of thinking, perceiving,
questioning are encouraged.
— MAYA ANGELOU

A CORPORATION IS a human body, according to the law. So it should come as no surprise that companies act very much like individuals. When people take good care of themselves, they are apt to be happy. Good outlooks actually change your looks. And when we get down in the dumps or trash ourselves, we feel like garbage.

Companies are no different, except that the head of the company often determines how all of its parts feel.

Chief executives who are hapless, hopeless, and helpless will send their companies into

depression. Leaders who are hopeful and visionary will take their companies to unexpected
heights.

Thinking is the determining factor. It will ultimately set the tenor, the environment, and the
expectations of everyone in the company. And,
like all thinking, it emanates from the head, so
let's start there.

WHAT STATE IS THE HEAD
OF STATE IN

Harry Truman said, "Being a president is like
riding a tiger. A man has to keep on riding or he
is swallowed." This attitude would guide him
and our country through the tumultuous years
at the close of World War II. John F. Kennedy
challenged America to put a man on the moon,
and that one call to action did as much to put a
man on the moon as NASA. And Martin Luther
King, Jr., said, "If a man hasn't discovered something that he will die for, he isn't fit to think."
The Head of State often determines our state of
mind.

Ronald Reagan made many of us feel great, as

IDEAS REACH NEW HEIGHTS

IN 1852, AMERICAN INVENTOR ELISHA GRAVES OTIS CREATED
THE FIRST ELEVATOR THAT WOULD NOT CRASH. TO PROVE ITS
SAFETY, HE HAD A PASSENGER TAKE THE ELEVATOR UP AND UP AND
UP. THEN HE HAD THE CABLE CUT. THE ELEVATOR DESCENDED
SLOWLY AND SAFELY. THE PASSENGER EXITED UNHARMED — BUT
NEVER HEARD OF AGAIN. THE INVENTOR'S LAST NAME, OTIS,
NOW APPEARS IN ELEVATORS ALL AROUND THE WORLD.

if there were a new day dawning in America. His incredible talent for telling a story motivated the nation like never before. It was his positive thinking that made all of us think differently.

Why do you think that Bill Clinton won against George Bush? It's simple. Bush might have won a war, but he lost the vision. While Bush talked about the mission of America, Clinton talked about destiny.

THE MISSION STATEMENT VS. THE DESTINY STATEMENT

Conventional businesses have mission statements. These documents usually appear in annual reports, bronze plaques, and corporate guideline manuals. You'll find other mission statements on the back of business cards and in restrooms.

I don't believe in mission statements, even though our company has one: *BrightHouse is the world's first Ideation Corporation. We create ideas that have enormous monetary value and sell these ideas to Chief Executives around the world.* Many mission statements seem to be alike and are very predictable: a statement of purpose, some values, and tons of commas.

Like a tombstone in a cemetery, the mission statement is unveiled, and then we visit it once a year. The reason most mission statements miss their mark is because they are not turned into action, and the reason for this is that most missions do not provoke enough thought.

A mission, by definition, is a religious quest, a doctrine to live and die by. American businesses that lose their way are founded on weak missions. What is needed are **destiny statements.**

When BrightHouse accepts a project, the first meeting we have is with our management and the chief executive of the new client. It is here that the CEO delivers his or her destiny. As opposed to focusing on the corporation's identity, the destiny focuses on the individual. What does he/she think about on the way home from work? What illumination has he/she had about the company? What will he/she do for the company and why? We ask them to imagine a future reality as opposed to their mission today. The result is two-fold: the destiny statement identifies (1) a direction, and (2) a purpose. From here we develop an action plan based on the chief executive's passion. Some want to go slow, some fast. Some want to create more value in the company by trimming down the company, while others want to create a values-based company where the bottom line is secondary to the employees.

Missions are determined, destinies are predetermined. Any fate other than success is unacceptable. Yet some CEOs want to maintain and some want to change. The smart ones want to create a revolution, and not a conventional one, either. The super CEOs want to create a perpetual revolution, believing that the future belongs to those who reinvent the game, not react to it.

When IBM was building Macro Hard, Bill Gates went Microsoft. Anita Roddick created the Body Shop when nobody was watching. Starbuck's percolated in someone's brain. The great CEOs have purpose, direction, and passion. Three years ago, our agency T-shirt read, "Passion Makes Perfect."

AFTER PASSION, COMPASSION

Today's thinking company is kinder and gentler. CEOs know that customers come second. It's the employee who comes first. In a way, the best CEOs work for their employees.

Thinking companies are bending over backwards to be more thoughtful. According to Joan Peters, when First Tennessee National Corporation trained one thousand of its managers in family support and allowed employees to create their own schedules, it retained staff twice as long. Aetna Insurance cut resignations in half by extending maternity leave to six months and saved a million dollars in hiring and training. IBM allows its employees to work part-time for up to three years and provides personal leave with health benefits. Xerox Corporation offers $10,000 in benefits to families in need of child care or college tuition. Microsoft has eliminated set hours for its telecommuters. Peters also points out that when the Lotus Development Corporation offered four weeks paid leave to new mothers and fathers, one-third of the applicants were men. Shorter work weeks and work days are just around the corner. People are turning in their bigger paychecks for bigger amounts of time with their families. They are thinking about what's important. And if they are not, chances are they are the wrong people.

One of the guidelines of BrightHouse is to hire "once-in-a-lifetime people." These include the curious, the odd, and the avant-garde. It is through them that conventional thinking is not only questioned but blown up.

When asked by a national beer company to develop a name and logo for a microbrewed beer to compete with other microbrews in the South, a young thinker had an idea of a bottle with no name or label. I heard about it and turned it over to our creative director to design the nameless and logoless bottle and then contacted the national beer company for a meeting as soon as possible. Forty-eight hours later, the prototype was presented: a long-neck beer bottle with no name or label. The only distinguishing feature was a painted red neck. (As Tom Peters suggests, "Weed out the dullards, nurture the nuts.")

HOW TO CREATE CREATIVE PEOPLE

I was once given a great piece of advice about running an organization: Always go to your staff's weddings and funerals. Though this sounds a bit crass, I think it's a great start. After all, those two are life events, and in today's thinking environment we don't create jobs, we create lives.

In addition to all conventional holidays and two-week vacations, everyone at BrightHouse receives their birthday off, March 4 off (the day we all march forth on our dreams), mental days (days for personal reflection), and the time between Christmas Eve and the first Monday after New Year's Day. This is a thinking corporation's vacation schedule, designed around the most important asset in today's corporation: thinkers.

I wasn't always this way. As chairman of the board and chief executive officer of Babbit & Reiman, my first company, I worked people day and night. We had a neon sign that hung in the window of the agency, so the entire city of Atlanta could see it. It read, "Open 25 hours a day." If you left before ten o'clock at night, you were given a frown by your fellow employees. I came in some mornings to find people strewn across the floor who had been working all night. We had an expression, "If you don't come in on Saturday, don't bother coming in on Sunday."

That, I guess, was the eighties, but I don't think you can run a genuinely thoughtful company that way for the long haul. BrightHouse closes at 5:30 every day — or at least we try. As opposed to my earlier corporate incarnations, we concentrate on quality hours versus the quantity of hours, on thought versus speed, on reputation versus money, and brains versus brawn. Thinkers think all the time, so as chief executive I need not keep my eyes on the watch. More important is to watch with my eyes. How do people feel? How are they interacting with one another? Are their personal destinies being fulfilled by BrightHouse?

Thought, as I've said before, speeds up as we slow down. The day of the client-imposed deadline is dead. After all, deadlines do not serve clients well. How creative can you be if you are ruled by something called a *deadline*? When clients say, "But I needed it yesterday," I know they're living in the past.

Our reputation for quality thinking is our purpose for being. No company should compromise its quality for money. The Almighty Dollar is no different from the Wizard of Oz; behind the curtain, the Almighty turns out to be a little money.

Hire brains. In the past, I never gave smarts the billing it gets today. Often a client would ask how many people were going to be working on the account, and I would answer six. Within a week six bodies would show up. Today, give me just one thinker. My clients agree.

FIREPROOF YOUR COMPANY

People who love to get fired up about their projects are the thoroughbreds of thinkers. But people who get fired up a lot also burn out more often. So a thinking company needs to find ways to fireproof itself.

TEN WAYS TO
FIREPROOF YOUR COMPANY

1. Spend time with every individual. Your time is part of their salary, not a bonus.
2. Taking the day *on* is more important than a day *off*. Encourage your staff to follow their dreams.
3. Demand that employees take vacation. At Hallmark, editors, writers, and illustrators get a paid week in a city such as London for creative renewal and inspiration.
4. Keep lots of fresh juice and fruit around to replenish your employees for the fruits of their labor.

5. Order fresh flowers every day and encourage everyone to take one flower home each night.

6. Reward miracles. BrightHouse donates a $500 savings bond to its employees' new additions.

7. Acknowledge people, not their jobs. Employees are not born into their jobs, and when they leave earth they can't take their titles with them. A job well done is really a person doing well.

8. Encourage lots of breaks. An accordion makes music when you push in both sides. But they have to go out.

9. Where there's smoke, there is fire. If a problem arises, come to the rescue ASAP.

10. Install a fire alarm. At BrightHouse we have a bell that people are expected to ring when they get hot around the collar. Ringing it acknowledges that they are aware of their own heat and signals the staff that he or she will deal with it. A calm will come over the office almost immediately.

Is the Flex Corporation Next?

Perhaps the best illustration of the latest thinking came from an assignment BrightHouse accepted from Randstad, the worldwide staffing corporation. They were looking for the next big idea in staffing, and President Erik Vonk and I met for lunch.

The Soulful Idea

HUMPHREY O'SULLIVAN OF BOSTON WAS DETERMINED TO FIND A JOB. HE WALKED THE STREETS DAY AFTER DAY. TIRED OF HIS SHOES TAKING A BEATING, HE INVENTED RUBBER SOLES.

Vonk's company has offices in virtually every country in the world. The U.S. market, of course, is critical for success, and, after swallowing a number of temporary services firms, he was ready to create the idea that would alter the shared reality of all people looking for work.

The idea architecture, or strategic blueprint, was developed by our COO and chief strategic counsel. He hypothesized that, unlike Boomers, Generation-Xers would want many jobs, not just one. They were looking for experiences instead of one job during their one life. Research showed that many college graduates expected to work in as many as nine different jobs during their career. The thinking here was a way to create their own life at their own speed. They wanted flexibility.

During incubation, BrightHouse developed the concept of Flexlife® for Ranstad. Like flextime, it allows people a flexible schedule. Only the schedule we were talking about here would be the calendars of their lives. In effect, Randstad offered new workers "a new way to work and live." This was the theme we developed, and now a book is being written by Eric Vonk entitled *Don't Get a Job, Get a Life*, which elaborates upon the idea. The value of the idea was acknowledged at a recent dinner with Vonk, who said, "Flexlife could add a half-billion dollars to our bottom line while helping people all over the world get their dream jobs."

It's always satisfying to do well and do good at the same time. But underlying this story is a lesson on establishing a creative thinking environment. Just as these future workers feel trepidation about working for one employer, they also don't like the idea of having one job. So today's creative thinking environment must challenge its inhabitants with more than just one job.

A MILLION FOR YOUR THOUGHTS

The age of "a penny for your thoughts" is coming to an end. Imagine this scenario. You write and direct your own film. It's a movie based on an idea Steven Spielberg gave to you. How much is his idea worth to the promotion of the film? Chances are the opening film credit would read "A Steven Spielberg Idea." Though "only" an idea, chances are it's a pretty good one. How much should Spielberg get for his idea? Not pennies but millions.

You, too, should receive credit for ideas. One day film credits will begin with an idea credit, but until then ideas must be treated like jewels.

In advertising, ideas are sold for nothing. Often agencies have to pay to create their ideas, and prospective clients just take a look and leave. The ideation firm does not give away these assets. Today our fee is $450,000 per idea. Some of our clients pay us a million dollars a year for our thinking. The price will only rise as people and companies realize that the real possessions are not material, but electrochemical events called *thought*.

We all know that one picture is worth a thousand words. The challenge for our society will be to create the axiom that "one thought is worth a thousand dollars." How much is seeing the light worth to a company or person in the dark?

INVASION OF THE BRAIN SNATCHERS

If you were afraid of "The Body Snatchers," get ready for the Brain Snatchers. You might be working with them. Many companies assume that all thinking that goes on within their four walls belongs to the company, not to the thinkers. Needless to say, this puts a crimp in the concept of creating value for your ideas and serves as a disincentive to smart thinking.

If I create an idea on my way to work, and my company owns that idea, that's analogous to their owning my mind. The brain-snatching policy needs to cease, and employees need to reclaim the ownership of their own ideas. One of my favorite golden rules is, "Treat other people's ideas as you would your own." There are other golden rules as well. Here are five I try to live by. All of them are about building a company that values and reward thinkers.

Turn your suggestion box into a suggestion company. The suggestion box to a company is what the big analog computers were to the military-industrial complex thirty years ago. They are outdated. We must think outside the box. That is, take those suggestions off the index cards and become suggestion people.

Give credit where credit is due. At Whirley

Industries, Inc., a family-owned business that manufactures plastic mugs and sports bottles, they have created a good idea club. Every employee is required to submit one good idea a month. The best ideas are rewarded with silver coins (gold if the idea is implemented) that can be redeemed for gasoline, pizza, or time off. The increases in productivity and profits have been phenomenal.

Pay handsome salaries for thinkers. This should go without saying but, in fact, often goes without being done. At too many companies, it's the great office politicians, the in-house schemers and self-promoters, who get ahead rather than those who have the best ideas. Part of every manager's job is to find out who really did the thinking, not who took credit for it. The best way to attract thinkers is to pay them. Be sure you do.

Give your thinkers plenty to think about. In every way possible, companies need to find ways to stimulate their employees. Since thinking need not be done at the office, stimulating travel experiences will be part of the thinkers' jobs. Outward Bound might open up a division called "Inward Bound," which trains people how to tap into their creativity.

Look for collaborators. The company of tomorrow will encourage investigation. It has to. Research and development will be augmented by up-to-the-second knowledge available on the Internet. But when it comes to pulling that research together, it will be a collaborative process. Tomorrow's best workers will be trained to work together, so collectively they can come up with much bigger and richer ideas than any one of them could produce on their own.

TOMORROW'S THINKING COMPANY IS MORE THOUGHTFUL

It's been said that intelligence is the ability to adapt. Nothing could be more true of companies today. Consumers are demanding it, and the companies thinking about their customers instead of themselves will be the winners of tomorrow.

By the twenty-first century, I imagine that all companies that make products will have to enter the service business. The mass market demands it. Quality is only the ticket into the arena. Service will be the determining factor between winners and losers. Commodities will become service-based, and the corporation as we know it today will become a service provider. Of course, the greatest service you can give a person is to think on their behalf.

If America wants to keep its competitive edge, we must become a thinking country. The company that thinks, reinvents, throws out convention, becomes knowledge-based, and delivers all the thinking it possibly can will win the customer's loyalty. This will demand a new moral for the corporation. Companies will have to be knowledge-based and consumer-driven. Most important, they must be personal.

Mass personalization is the ability to reach the

masses one by one. "One size fits all" will be replaced by "Your size fits you." Because of technology, companies can now fit you individually by computer whether you're buying a pair of jeans or a bicycle.

In the book *The Virtual Corporation* by William H. Davidow and Michael S. Malone, I found some startling data on the speed with which the Japanese develop new cars. From design to delivery, a Japanese car takes forty-six months and $1.7 million in engineering hours as opposed to sixty months and $3 million in the United States. The Japanese spend less time researching cars and more time responding to the needs of their customers. I guess that's what is meant by "A simple idea from Honda," which, by the way, became the best-selling car in the United States.

In order to attract consumers who are growing less loyal everyday, companies will have to become more flexible. Consumers will demand that today's insurance company become tomorrow's full-service financial company.

Doctors today are being forced to become more holistic. We are not far off from an integrated Western and Eastern medical practice. Don't be surprised in the future to see the A.H.H.A. — the American Holistic Healing Association. It will happen. Tax firms are turning into financial services firms and movie theaters are turning into theme parks.

The thinking corporation is nimbler, smarter, and weighs less. It's a gazelle among dinosaurs. It can be torn down and built up overnight, should the need arise. And the need has arisen.

THE WORLD
IDEA NETWORK

Great thinkers think inductively, that is, they create the solution and then seek out the problems that solution might solve; most companies think deductively, that is, defining a problem and then investigating different solutions.

Like Navy Seals, thinkers are trained to think before they fight. They have been trained to attack the future. All companies in the future will have these kinds of thinkers, or they will not survive.

Finally, I would like to share a story about my friend, Michael Greenlees. When he started GGT advertising on Dean Street in London, England, back in the early 1980s, he believed his destiny would be to make enough money to create an advertising network that would attract blue-chip companies, and then he would sell them intellectual capital or ideas.

Today, Michael Greenlees will tell you that his real destiny was to be part of the growing

---

AN IDEA TO SLEEP ON

KEMMONS WILSON, A SMALL CONTRACTOR IN MEMPHIS, TENNESSEE, WANTED TO STAY IN A HOTEL NEAR A HIGHWAY WITH ADEQUATE PARKING BUT WITHOUT A TRUMPED-UP LOBBY AND A FRU-FRU DINING ROOM ASSOCIATED WITH HOTELS OF THE TIME. HE DECIDED THE WORLD NEEDED SOMETHING HE CALLED A "MOTEL." AFTER ALL, THE HIGH SCHOOL DROPOUT KNEW NOTHING ABOUT HOTELS. ALL HE HAD WAS A BELIEF, INSTILLED IN HIM BY HIS MOTHER, THAT HE COULD CREATE ANYTHING IN THE WORLD. WITHIN A FEW YEARS, WILSON HAD BUILT WHAT WOULD BECOME THE LARGEST MOTEL CHAIN IN THE WORLD. NEXT TIME YOU'RE AT A HOLIDAY INN, REMEMBER KEMMONS.

vanguard of ideators who know the opposite to be true.

First, you must have intellectual capital. Blue-chip companies will flock to this wealth of knowledge, and because the demand will be high for those ideas, a network will be built. And as a byproduct of this Worldwide Idea Network, or W.I.N., the bottom line grows commensurate with the value of the idea.

Ideas create everything.

Like the Wallis and BrightHouse models, the company of tomorrow will encourage investigation. Employees will be encouraged to investigate and perfect their talents and to enlarge their domains. Up-to-the-second information from the library and the Internet and responses from appropriate psychographic and demographic audiences will become as crucial as the assembly line used to be. Research will be replaced with the search to obtain meaningful, timely information rather than a history lesson.

Incubation will be lengthened as companies charge for their thinking. Downtime will be thought of as uptime. More and more people will realize that deep thinking is the most lucrative kind. Financial meditation will replace speedy advice, producing more thoughtful possibilities rather than canned plans. Time planners, a division of human resources, will ensure "quantity control" — the amount of time needed to think.

A new line of aroma products that might be called Common Scents will permeate hallways to stimulate or calm brain activity. Music, as well, will be part of everyone's thinking arsenal.

Sanctuaries — places of prayer — will have a new place in tomorrow's companies. Today many companies already pray together before the start of the work day. However, with the advent of "looking for divine inspiration," work and prayer will come closer together. At work, this will mean not just a focus on spiritual values, but the value of spiritual pursuits and their effect on inspiration. The Bible will move from the hotel side table to center screen on our computer terminal.

Ideas will become more important than innovations, and a job well done will be an illumination, a discovery. That shift will capture the imagination of everyone in the company, especially since it was a collaborative effort. People will be trained to work together in an effort to produce a much bigger idea than any one member of the team could produce on his or her own. Warren Bennis calls it "voluntary mutual responsibility." Tomorrow it will be called TeamPlay, which has replaced teamwork.

Once people get the idea, illustration houses will open all over the country. They will start as photo centers and Kinko's-like concepts and then grow into multinational corporations that produce ideas in the forms of comprehensive programs, pictures, words, lights, and sounds.

Famed advertising czar Bill Bernbach (the co-creator of the original Volkswagen campaign, "Think small"), of Doyle, Dane, Bernbach Advertising said that, "Perfect execution can become the idea itself." His prophecy will come true as these execution houses translate ideas into perfect reality. In the end, I predict, these execution and illustration houses will enter into an alliance with manufacturers. This could turn the Kinko's of today into an IBM of tomorrow.

The most important change of all will be the notion that the real asset of brain power will be held by its owner and the company that contracts for its use. Talent brokers will offer your skills to specified projects and missions. Companies will expand and attract based on the level of think power needed. Like the all-star teams of baseball and basketball, the best and the brightest people will be enlisted to win the games of science, arts, and humanities every day.

Does this sound utopian? Maybe it does. But who's to say that utopias won't ever exist? I'm betting that they will and that today's business paradigm of companies that do it "faster, cheaper, and better" will be replaced by a new paradigm of thinking companies that offer "slower, more expensive, and best."

Furthermore, tomorrow's true economy will not rise and fall like today's stock market but will go up and down as we ride the office elevator every day.

A MATCHLESS IDEA

ENGLISH CHEMIST JOHN WALKER NEVER PATENTED HIS INVENTION — MATCHES — BECAUSE HE SAID IT WAS TOO IMPORTANT AN IDEA. HIS PROFITS WENT UP IN SMOKE. MARCEL BICH, WHO INVENTED DISPOSABLE LIGHTERS, KNEW HIS IDEA WAS BIG. AS A RESULT HE SET THE INDUSTRY ON FIRE AND PROFITED HANDSOMELY.

CHAPTER 8

THE THINKING LIFE

*"What lies behind us and what lies
before us are tiny matters compared
to what lies within us."*
— OLIVER WENDELL HOLMES

THOUGHTS THAT ENLIGHTEN the soul are more precious than jewels. These gems give our lives meaning and keep us from getting trapped in the muck of small thoughts and petty dreams. But how much do most of us know about the organ that does the thinking — our brain? How much do we know about keeping this instrument of thinking physically and mentally tuned? If we're going to be thinkers, it makes sense to learn as much as we can about just how that thinking gets done.

The ancient Indians, Egyptians, and Chinese didn't think much about the brain. The brain, most believed, had little to do with thinking. Aristotle speculated that the brain was a cooling system for blood on its way to and from the heart. As for thought, though, in his *Metaphysics* he wrote, "It is of itself that the divine thought thinks and its thinking is the thinking on thinking." Then Plato threw in his two cents, hypothesizing that reasoning faculties were housed in our heads. What followed were a number of individuals who concluded that the seat of the soul was actually located between our two ears. Nothing really changed in the way of major progress in what would become the field of neuroscience for fifteen hundred years.

Over the last three decades, an enormous amount of knowledge has been collected, but the brain is still far from being completely understood. Each human brain contains more than ten billion neurons. That's more than twice the number of people on this planet. These neurons are connected by fibers. The junction that connects neurons is called the synapse. Only a few thousandths of an inch across, these junctions are the most important part of your nervous system. Add in the one hundred billion glial cells that surround your neurons delivering nourishment and insulation, and you've got something to think about.

THE IDEA THAT MAKES PROFITS
FOR THE PROPHETS

THE CASSETTE-DRIVER MECHANISM, SUPERMARKET BARCODE SCANNER, FAX MACHINE, AND THE SONY WALKMAN ARE BUT A FEW OF THE FIVE HUNDRED PATENTS UNDER HIS NAME. WITH THE MONEY HE MADE, HE SET UP A FOUNDATION THAT AWARDS $500,000 A YEAR TO AMERICAN INVENTORS. WHAT MAKES THE NAME JEROME H. LEMELSON SO SPECIAL, THOUGH, WAS PERHAPS HIS BIGGEST IDEA — TO AWARD THE HALF MILLION TO INVENTORS WHO NEVER SHARED IN THE PROFITS DERIVED FROM THEIR WORK.

Although only 2 to 3 percent of the body is made up of the brain, our gray matter consumes 20 percent of our oxygen intake.

The brain is divided into the brain stem, the cerebellum, and the cerebrum, but there are two main parts. There is the left side of the brain, with linear, analytical, and logical functions, and the right side, which concentrates more on spatial abilities and creative thinking.

Most of us in the United States use the left side of our brain more than the right. This is the result, I believe, of our educational system and the fact that our country has always embraced the left-brain culture.

When I went to grammar school, junior high, and high school, art was taught once or, at the most, twice a week. No one even imagined classes teaching creative thinking. In hindsight, this has caused real problems for most of us today. The right side of our brains has never been fully developed. If you believe, as I do, that your "gut" resides on the right side, then your intuitive reasoning has also been shortchanged.

PICTURE THIS

Etymologically, an idea is the "look" of something. The word idea comes ultimately from the same source as the Greek verb *idein* or "to see." People, in fact, see their ideas. Visions don't come in headlines. They are pictures that are created inside our heads.

The proverbial lightbulb that goes off inside your head is actually a mental flashlight. Whatever you do, don't think of a pink elephant.

Now that you see a pink elephant, you know what I mean.

So if an idea is the look of something — if the word means "to see" — then one way to think up great ideas is *to see* them as opposed to *thinking of* them. Seeing things a different way is what great ideas are all about. How many times, when asked a question, have you responded with, "Let's see . . ."? That's the beginning. Now you need to go sight-seeing. Often, I think of my mind as a travel agency that can send me anywhere in the world and outside the world, too. This book's dust jacket is an illustration of the limitlessness of what I'm talking about. That man sees everything.

See? You did.

Betty Edwards is author of *Drawing On the Right Side of the Brain* and *Drawing On the Artist Within*, which focuses on the right and left hemispheres' roles in creativity. She cites our educational system's ignorance, to some degree abhorrence, of cultivating creativity through art. "The result is that the key aspect of the brain's potential — the right hemisphere — is vastly underutilized. The result is bizarre," Edwards says. "People who cannot draw tend to avoid taking drawing classes. This is like choosing not to take a French class because you don't know how to speak French."

Edwards theorized that if we could find a way into our right hemisphere, we could discover a whole new way of thinking. She developed exercises that include close attention to complex visual details and open-ended time commitment. The left brain wants to get out quick. Seen from the left side of the brain, life becomes a series of *Cliff Notes* books, as opposed to the right brain that loves to marinate in the nuances of life itself.

Tony Schwartz, who wrote the wonderful book *What Really Matters: Search for Wisdom in America*, took a drawing course from Edwards and was delighted with the result. Not only was he able to draw a self-portrait but was powerfully impacted by the experience with her. He remembers, "She creates a nurturing, non-judgmental environment in which the expectation for success is high and the possibility of failure never enters the picture. . . . Put another way, the right hemisphere mode is a fragile and elusive state that can easily be overridden by the left hemisphere's rush to judgment."

All my early life my mother tried to create a nurturing environment in which my mind could play. Her big rule was "Never lose in your imagination." She told me that thoughts were things and that I would become the thing I thought of most. This kind of empowerment is crucial to creative thinking.

The stages of incubation and illumination are, as Edwards suggests, preeminently right-brain skills. Investigation and illustration, that is, gathering information and translating the idea into a form that can be understood, are functions of the left brain.

So it seems that if you want to be a great thinker, you need to use both sides of your brain. For you left-brain analytical types, you might want to take an art course, and you right-brainers might want to balance the family checkbook more often.

We all need to practice holistic thinking, combining both sides, taking into account what we don't see as much as what we do see.

A BETTER SCHOOL OF THINKING

It won't be enough, however, to master the act of thinking. Structure follows substance. Our education system needs to be overhauled. The Galloway School in Atlanta is one such place where students play the game of learning rather than the game of school.

I've learned a great deal from Dr. Linda Martinson, headmaster of Galloway, who believes that learning should be collaborative, not competitive.

In a way, Galloway is an ideation education. Plato predicted this long ago: "Do not then train youths to learning by force and harshness, but direct them to it by what amuses their minds so that you may be better able to discover with accuracy the peculiar bent of the genius of each."

If there's been an idea downsizing in this country, it's because our education system has failed our children. Classrooms must be filled with excitement, playfulness, and security as well as education. Indeed, the real road to a democratic society begins with a democratic education system. One of the great things about ideas is that they are nondiscriminatory and nondenominational. Great thinkers don't need high IQs. To the extent that IQ means anything, and I'm not sure it does, it certainly doesn't mean ideas quotient. The average college student has an IQ of 120, which is more than enough to create a breakthrough idea in any endeavor.

What we need is an education system that truly teaches and rewards thinking, not memorization. John Dewey, the turn-of-the-century education visionary, believed that people must teach children to think, not what to think. According to Isabelle Buckley in *College Begins at Two*, there are too many toys that have been created to teach skills as opposed to stimulate imaginations.

If we really want a democratic society, I've got a two-part plan to get us there. First, we reward and nuture ideas. Second, we create a school system that teaches everyone how to think creatively. Suddenly, the gaps between rich and poor, haves and have-nots, begin to wither. As Gloria Bromell-Tinubu of Spelman College told me, "If, in fact, we provide an education for all, making it accessible to all, and providing the quality of education that will encourage the kind of idea production that we're talking about, then that levels the playing field. It doesn't matter if you are black or white, male or female, old or young, living in this country or some other country. You are in a position to own your intellectual capital and be a property owner, and in that sense engage and have protective property rights that you can then use to your benefit and to society's benefit."

THE HIGHER SCHOOL OF UNLEARNING

Most of us need to unlearn the basic tenants ingrained in us and reteach ourselves to think intuitively, creatively, and naturally.

Again, most schools teach us that the chicken crossed the road to get to the other side. So it's not surprising that when given a problem, most of us will try to come up with an answer that offers previous solutions and reports filled with proven answers and data. This breaks all the rules of great thinking.

After graduating from high school and college, most of us stop learning. We are chickens, and we pick up our diploma on the other side of the road. But lifelong learning is essential for great thinking.

Everyone needs to go to an art museum at least once a month. One of our clients, the Metropolitan Museum of Art in New York City, houses our entire civilization under one roof. Go to a play or a concert once a month. Live theater is experiential: it will change your behavior. Buy a book once a week and read it. Be sure to read outside your interests, go to plays outside your liking, listen to music you've never heard before, and see art you know nothing about. Knowledge that is not immediately useful will add to your course in lifelong learning.

THE MOST NATURAL IDEA OF ALL

AUTHOR HENRY DAVID THOREAU SPENT MORE THAN TWO YEARS IN THE WOODS CONNECTING WITH THE BIRDS, THE TREES, AND HIMSELF. HE FELT THAT A LIFE VOID OF MATERIAL PURSUITS WOULD PROVIDE A MORE FRUITFUL EXPERIENCE. AND IT DID. FROM HIS MASSACHUSETTS CABIN ON WALDEN POND, THIS DIF- FERENT DRUMMER PRODUCED NOT JUST A LIFETIME OF GREAT WORK BUT A PHILOSOPHY ON HOW TO HAVE A GREAT LIFE. "YOU MUST GET YOUR LIVING BY LOVING."

Perhaps one day we will be able to enroll in the unlearning institute and relearn how to glean what life has to offer us on the road as opposed to the other side of it. **Knowledge is not a destination, it's a journey.** One might call it an "edventure."

Roland S. Barth, founding director of the Principal's Center and lecturer of education at the Harvard College School of Education, noted recently, "It's been estimated that fifty years ago high school students graduated knowing perhaps 75 percent of what they needed to know in the workplace. Today, the estimate is that graduates of our schools leave knowing perhaps 2 percent of what they will need to know. Ninety-eight percent is yet to come."

Imagine a chicken in great haste to get to the other side of the road. Between him and his goal are a million moments of life he could enjoy. However, all that is on his mind is the ludicrous pecking order of success. From womb to tomb, all he wants is to get to the other side. What's lost is life itself. At the very least, this is one stressed chicken.

STRESS — THE GREAT BRAIN DRAIN

Stress destroys everything, and it's rampant today. According to the Yankelovich Monitor, America's preeminent trends analysis firm, stress is society's monster, creating havoc across all generations; 81 percent of those surveyed by Yankelovich are "screaming for stress relief." Stress is created from a lack of control, so anything you can't cope with causes stress on your brain as well as the rest of your body. In the brain-rich book *Brain Longevity*, Dharma Singh Khalsa points out, "If you can control a difficult situation, it will probably be good for your brain . . . loss of control drastically increases stress, and predictability of stress vastly reduces his or her stress response."

Creating a nonstressful environment for your brain is essential to healthy thinking.

A HEALTHY BRAIN IS A WEALTHY BRAIN

I've developed my own diet to keep stress down and my spirits up. I call it the Thinker's Diet, or How to Take the Weight of the World Off Your Shoulders.

1. *Pray for happiness.* Prayer works. I pray for health, wealth, and happiness. I talk to God when I pray. I listen to God when I meditate. I look for signs from God. To me, coincidence is just God's way of staying anonymous. The power of prayer is well documented as a healer. Prayer in many cases precedes the cure. As for thinking, I pray for good thoughts. And I thank God for everything. I even thank God for God.

2. *Keep what's important important.* There's a big difference between a lump in your cereal and a lump in your breast. It's okay to want success and things as long as you know most of the stuff (money, fame, etc.) are meaningless. I still haven't seen a hearse with a U-Haul behind it.

3. *Lower your expectations.* Should you feel stress coming your way because something

might not work out the way you want it to, just lower your expectations of the outcome. You'll feel yourself content even in a losing situation.

4. *Have a schedule.* The brain loves a map. "Life is what happens while you're making other plans," John Lennon sings. But a schedule or action plan gives you a sense of control, and that cuts stress in half. As Wordsworth once said, "To steer is heaven, to drift is hell."

5. *Be passionate.* Work and play demand all you've got, and when you lose yourself in the experience of life, you gain control and feel very happy. Mihaly Csikszentmihalyi, also author of the well-known book *Flow*, describes the word as the optimal state of inner harmony when all thoughts, feelings, senses, and actions are focused on the same goal. The process becomes so much more important than the outcome, so incredible, in fact, that the activity feels spontaneous and automatic. It's a state of bliss brought on by a passionate flow.

6. *Be your authentic self.* Only one of you has been made and for a very good reason. The world isn't finished yet, and we need you. Being your authentic self will allow your brain to expand exponentially. The only thing more important is *to be okay* with your authentic self. Creating yourself will lead to true happiness.

7. *Exercise your body.* I jump rope three times a week. Ten minutes of skipping rope can equal a thirty-minute run. It elevates your heart rate and is good for your head as well. If you want to learn the ropes to happiness, buy a jump rope. Remember, exercise actually makes your brain grow and increases cognitive power.

I meditate while jumping rope, imagining that my body, mind, and spirit are participating in a relay. After fifteen minutes of jumping, my body gives the baton to my mind. After forty-five minutes, my mind hands it over to my spirit.

8. *Slow your mind.* As I've mentioned earlier, slowing the mind down creates creativity. Of the four brain waves — beta, alpha, theta, and delta — alpha waves are present when daydreaming and visualizing. Theta waves reflect the brain state between wakefulness and sleep. It is in this state where we can tap into our repository of high creativity. It's no surprise that theta waves are two to four times slower than beta waves. One way to get there is described by the Buddhist and Vietnamese meditation teacher Thich Nhat Hanh:

> *My dear friends, suppose someone is holding a pebble and throws it in the air and the pebble begins to fall down into a river. After the pebble touches the surface of the water, it allows itself to sink slowly into the river. It will reach the bed of the river without any effort. Once the pebble is at the bottom of the river, it continues to rest. It allows the water to pass by.*
>
> *I think the pebble reaches the bed of the river by the shortest path because it allows itself to fall without making any effort. During our sitting meditation, we can allow ourselves to rest like a pebble. We can allow ourselves to sink naturally without effort to the position of sitting, the position of resting.*
>
> *Resting is a very important practice; we have to learn the art of resting. Resting is the first part of Buddhist meditation. You should allow your*

THINKING FOR A LIVING — 149

body and your mind to rest. Our mind as well as
our body needs to rest.

Oftentimes, meditation can be more beneficial than medication. When you meditate, you stop the whirlings of your mind. Your brain will thank you. As Robert Louis said, "Quiet minds cannot be perplexed or frightened, but go on in fortune or misfortune at their own private pace like a clock in a thunderstorm." What's more, meditation demands that you become consious of your breathing. While you're thinking about that, remember that the definition of *inspire* is "to breathe in."

9. *Stay connected.* Anything that connects heals. Anything that separates hurts. Gossip if you must, but stay connected at all costs. Physiologically, thinking is all about making connections in your head. Life is no different — when we connect, we think and feel better. When you hate someone, they live rent free in your head. When you love someone, the property between your ears goes up in value. Thinking about love is healthy.

10. *A sound mind is a happy mind.* Mozart's music "may warm up" the brain, suggests Gordon Shaw, a theoretical physicist. He says that complex music actually facilitates certain complex neuronal patterns. Scientists at the University of Washington found that the accuracy of ninety copy editors increased 21.3 percent when they listened to light classical music. What's more, thirty-six undergraduates at the University of California listened to ten minutes of Mozart's "Sonata for Two Pianos in D Major" (K. 448) and scored eight to nine points

higher on their spatial IQ tests. Should you come to my house or office, you'll hear classical music playing most of the time. It's music to my gears. In a recent article, Don Campbell, who is a trained classical musician, composer, and author of groundbreaking books on music and healing, also recommends Gregorian chants for meditating and reducing stress. Schubert, Schumann, Tchaikovsky, Chopin, and Liszt can enhance compassion. To uplift your spirits, turn on jazz, the blues, soul, calypso, and reggae; and to stimulate movement and release tension, nothing beats the King — Elvis. To create feelings of deep peace, religious music helps us transcend.

FOOD FOR THOUGHT

I'm not a doctor or an expert on pharmacology, but experts see the problems and solutions the same way.

Dharma Singh Khalsa, M.D., gives his readers a breakthrough medical program that improves their minds and memory. The diet includes a group of principles that I found incredibly helpful. Here they are:

Eat low-fat food. The doctor feels that what helps the heart helps the head. He believes that fat "rots your brains."

Eat a nutrient-dense diet. Nonfoods are out of the question, due to the brain's insatiable desire for a variety of nutrients. If the food isn't rich in nutrients, you're faking out the brain.

Avoid hypoglycemia. Glucose is fuel for the brain. When your blood sugar is low, your brain's motor functions poorly. Remember the word *diet* has the word *die* in it.

Eat a relatively low-calorie diet. Cut down your caloric intake and the doctor claims you'll add years to your brain. Rats and other animals have increased lifespans of up to 50 percent when their calorie-intake is reduced.

Eat a balanced diet. Khalsa points out that a balanced meal doesn't mean equal amounts of the four food groups. That's the imbalanced, high-fat style that's caused our country's waistline to expand. He suggests a diet of whole grains, vegetables, fruits, and nonanimal-based proteins.

Take supplements. A good diet is not good enough to regenerate your brain.

Eat real food. Processed foods are not part of the process for a healthy brain, and pesticides poison food. The doctor recommends real food, which is mostly food in the produce section.

Feed your neurotransmitters. The brain's chemical messengers — neurotransmitters — carry thoughts

---

A NOVEL IDEA FOR THINKING

CHARLES DICKENS, AUTHOR OF MANY GREAT NOVELS, WOULD SLEEP ONLY WITH HIS HEAD FACING NORTH. HE FELT THAT THE MAGNETIC FORCES WOULD AFFECT THE DIRECTIONS OF HIS LIFE AND CAREER, AN IDEA THAT APPARENTLY WORKED FOR HIM.

from one brain cell to another, affecting your memory, learning, energy, and happiness. When you feed them with such things as choline and serotonin, your brain gets a boost. Be sure to consult your physician or a nutritionist before you feed your head.

Khalsa adds that for brain stimulation we should eat protein, and for brain relaxation we should eat carbohydrates. A high-protein breakfast will keep a brain on its toes. For lunch, high protein beats high carbohydrates. How many of us have felt like going to the land of nod after lunch? Save it for dinner, Khalsa says. "Carbohydrates will increase your tryptophan uptake, and you'll soon be manufacturing the calming serotonin." Apparently, if you've got enough serotonin, you've got it made when it comes to sleep.

As for brain vitamins, here's a capsulated version of smart vitamins. Vitamin A protects the brain cells from free radicals. A B12 shortage reduces reasoning skills. B6 declines after age forty and is needed for optimal cognitive skills. B1 helps B6 to be more efficient and also combats the effects of alcohol. Folic acid has been helping with depression. Niacin helps to manufacture neurotransmitters. Remember B5, which is vital to the synthesis of the brain's primary memory neurotransmitter. Vitamin C is by far the winner when it comes to longevity, and in one study, it raised students' IQ tests by an average of five points. Vitamin E protects neurons and restores damaged neurotransmitter receptor sites and significantly slows brain aging.

As for minerals, selenium and zinc are both

THINKING FOR A LIVING — 153

crucial for maximum brain function, as are a number of amino acids.

As you can see, taking care of the brain takes brains, and buying Dr. Dharma Singh Khalsa's book would serve you well. You'll find the doctor's recommended dosages and much more.

Dr. Andrew Weil, author of a library of valuable books including the best-seller *Spontaneous Healing*, also offers a plethora of information on the relationship between the brain and the rest of your life.

Both Weil and Khalsa recommend ginko biloba for improved mental function. Weil reports that "many people report both physical and mental improvement after using this remedy for at least two months." Ginkgo biloba is the earth's longest-living tree. Each can have a lifespan of more than one thousand years.

On my shelf at the office is an idea waiting to happen. It's a line of fruit-based drinks with ginko biloba mixed in to get your creative juices going. Hopefully, this brain beverage will stimulate the mind in lieu of coffee. Coffee does aid thought and memory if it is not over consumed. I prefer green tea because it gives my brain the caffeine boost but also boosts my antioxidant war chest and decreases my chances of stroke.

AROMATHERAPY MAKES SCENTS FOR THINKING

The other day I dropped off my four-year-old son, Alden, at school. As I escorted him down the corridor, the smells of chalk mixed with hints of Playdough and a pinch of fingerpaint sent my mind back to Miss Wollack's first grade class. This memory took me back to a very creative time in my life.

Playdough has a special effect on me, as does talcum powder, the number one scent in the world.

Recent research shows that the properties of many scents, such as peppermint, basil, clove, and ylang-ylang, help stimulate the nervous system and energize mental activity. In Japan, peppermint is often pumped throughout offices to keep employees sharp.

Smells are passed directly to the limbic system brain, evoking an immediate emotional or instinctual response. Going back to grammar school isn't the only way to stimulate your brain. Try investigating essential oils at a health food store.

INSTANT MOTIVATORS

In my book *The Best Year of Your Life*, I offer 365 instant motivators. Here's a sample:

1. Give your mind a positive charge every morning by thinking a positive thought.
2. Put an upbeat message on your answering machine, such as, "This machine records only good news."
3. Set yourself a goal and write it on a small card. Now laminate it. Keep this card next to your driver's license so you'll never forget where you're going.
4. Think of your goal as a Federal Express package, as something that absolutely, positively has to be there.

5. Make a tape with your own voice telling yourself what you want out of life. Play it back once a week.

6. Place a red carpet beside your bed so that when you wake up in the morning, you will remember how people should treat you the rest of the day.

HOME IS WHERE THE HEAD IS

In Robert Fulghum's collection of writings entitled *Words I Wish I Wrote*, I found this piece of dialogue:

"Where's home for you?" A stranger asks a fellow traveler on a plane. "Wherever she is," comes the reply, as the man points at his wife.

This is how I think about my wife. If I had one secret for thinking, it would be in loving. A good thinker is a good lover. He loves music, art, the humanities, the sciences, all of his senses, and he loves the ability to take all the words and turn them into pictures and put it all into one, beautiful thought. But most of all, he must love someone else. For when we love, we practice love and ignite our passions.

Passion, together with imagination and belief, leads to great thinking. Passion starts you and sustains you. Imagination is the coal that makes the fire burn brighter, and belief is knowing that the idea will be created. Ideas love to be loved and cradled like a baby. They need nurturing, and the art of nurturing is learned at home. I know I am debunking the myth that sorrow and grief make for great creativity. By no means do I wish to discredit the Edgar Allen Poes or Sylvia Plaths of the world. I just believe from what I've learned and experienced that a loving home is a great starting point for thinking. **The road to success just might be your driveway.**

THINKING IS THE ART OF CONNECTING

You can't think smart if you don't live smart. That's why I always try to think first of my wife and children. After all, they will be what lasts.

Prominent educator Renate Caine points out in her book *Making Connections* that breakthroughs in neuroscience show that the brain is a social organ, that we learn best from one another. The brain seeks connections to what it already knows, especially as we grow older, thus supporting interactive learning and integrated curricula.

People who think together stick together. And it all starts when you meet your soul mate. It is here that the thinking must be started. Aristotle would have thought, "two bodies and one soul." Nothing much has changed since his time except for the fact that we don't think much about it. Like advertising, Western society has put more emphasis on the execution of a relationship than on the idea.

For too many, the idea of a covenant has become a contract full of ridiculous stipulations. Most of the thinking that goes into weddings revolves around caterers, food, and honeymoons.

In India the wedding ceremony takes three days. This is to ensure that the glue dries. Watching the rate of divorce in the Western world, you'd think most marriages are held together by Silly Putty. If we are to ever dedicate our minds to one thing, it should be creation, and creation begins with two people.

MY PROPOSAL

My most brilliant achievement was the ability to be able to persuade my wife to marry me.
— SIR WINSTON CHURCHILL

I'm not saying that I know any more about love and marriage than anyone else. However, when someone asks me what my greatest idea was, only one comes to mind — my family.

It all started when I was trying to get votes. Not for myself, but for Atlanta mayoral candidate Maynard Jackson. My firm had been hired to help him win the election.

I thoroughly enjoy political campaigns and creating ideas for them. Most recently I wrote the successful slogan, "Take Georgia to the Max," for now Senator Max Cleland. By the way, Senator Cleland won with the biggest idea since FDR's New Deal, and that was a positive campaign.

Maynard Jackson's campaign for mayor of Atlanta was a victory, too. The new mayor was incredibly gracious and thankful. He said to me, "Should I ever be able to help you, just let me know." Some of the greatest thinking is associative. That is when one thought leads you to another. Thomas Edison claims inventing the lightbulb was an eighteen-hundred-step process.

During the election I had been introduced to Cynthia Good, at that time a TV news anchor for CBS. She was beautiful, and her mind worked better than anyone's I had ever met. I guess journalists are by nature passionate and curious, but she was magical, too. I wanted to share the rest of my life with her. It wouldn't be the first life, either. I didn't meet Cynthia. I recognized her. I couldn't think of anyone or anything, only her.

Our courtship tested our wills, our memories, and our expectations of one another. But, like two kids copying off each other's test papers, we aced the exams.

Now it was time to propose, and I had to create an idea that would demonstrate all the skills I had ever learned. My first was associative. Mayor Jackson did say that he would help me, so I called him. And I also called the Japanese firm that owned Atlanta's tallest building, the IBM tower. And I called CBS, and I called the caterers, and I called in three producers from my agency.

Just before the six o'clock news, Cynthia received a message from her news director that a

---

He Wouldn't Accept Dirt for an Idea

Don't expect to shake this man's hand upon meeting him. And, should you invite him for dinner, expect him to wipe all the silverware and plates. One can only conclude that his obsessive fear of dirt and infection led Louis Pasteur to create the process of pasteurization.

white-collar drug bust was about to go down in the penthouse of the IBM tower in midtown Atlanta. The police chief had been told to give Cynthia Good the exclusive story. The news director told her it would be the lead story, live, and that she should hightail it down to the tower to get the story.

Leading two camera trucks, Cynthia Good raced to the intersection of Peachtree and 14th Street where she witnessed some twenty police cars surrounding the building, a SWAT team, and a fire truck (I couldn't swing the chopper).

Cynthia demanded to be let into the building. She was told, "Sorry, ma'am, no one goes in. This is a very dangerous situation." But Cynthia persevered and finally prevailed. Except for one last catch: a Red Dog SWAT team would have to escort her to the fiftieth floor, which it did. Once there, they broke down the door.

Behind it, she found not a Colombian drug cartel but a knight of sorts — me — and dinner, champagne, and musicians playing as the sun sank behind the picture windows, and I sank to my knees. She sank, too. And we've been afloat ever since.

Our marriage has brought with it an evolution of our thinking. After all, ideation is Darwinian. Only the fittest ideas survive and prosper. Two of our ideas would be the greatest ever.

How to Conceive a Baby

First, you must think about your future child as demonstrated by a wonderful story from Jack Cornfield's book, *A Path with Heart*.

> In a tribe in East Africa, the birthdate
> of a child is not counted from the day
> of its physical birth, nor even the day
> of conception, as in the other villages.
> For this tribe the birthdate comes the
> first time the child is thought of in its
> mother's mind. Aware of her inten-
> tion to conceive a child with a partic-
> ular father, the mother then goes off
> to sit alone under a tree. There she
> sits and listens until she can hear the
> song of the child that she hopes to
> conceive. Once she has heard it, she
> returns to her village and teaches it to
> the father so that they can sing it
> together as they make love, inviting
> the child to join them. The song will
> follow them through all the cere-
> monies of his life until it is sung one
> more time at his death.

Thinking together creates intimacy, which is
the whole idea of marriage. My family has been
my support. They are my Dream Team. They
have helped me create an environment where we
can grow and cultivate ideas.

Recently I was given a project by the Georgia-
Pacific Corporation. While teaching my four-
year-old son the meaning of recycling, I picked
up a used core of bathroom tissue. Alden and I
went out and bought some seeds, which we then
embedded in the cardboard core. When recy-
cled, the core would yield new life, new trees for
the future. I presented the idea to Georgia-

Pacific, and they loved it. Alden loved it, too. He wanted to know if angels made trees grow. I assured him that they do.

* * *

We are what we think
All that arises with our thoughts
With our thoughts we make the world
Speak or act with an impure mind,
And trouble will follow you.
As the wheel follows the ox that draws
the cart
We are what we think
All that arises with our thoughts
With our thoughts we make the world
Speak or act with a pure mind,
And happiness will follow you.
As your shadow, unshakable.

"Teachings from the Buddha"
From *A Path with Heart*
by Jack Cornfield

CHAPTER 9

"I THINK, THEREFORE I AM VALUABLE"

"I paid Joey Reiman
$1 million just to think."
— JIM ADAMSON
PRESIDENT, CEO, AND CHAIRMAN OF
ADVANTICA RESTAURANT GROUP

WE HAVE THE same birthday — March 31. Sure, it was 357 years before mine, but that's enough of a link for me to explore this great French mathematician and philosopher's way of thinking.

René Descartes was not satisfied to believe only what he was taught. He questioned everything until he could prove it true or false. What's more, the only thing he knew to be true without any doubt was that he was alive, and the only way he knew that was through thinking. He summed up his philosophy with the phrase, "I think, therefore I am."

Basically, Descartes was looking for truth. That was his principle interest in life, and if you think about it, it's most of ours, too. Higher education is driven by the search for truth. Harvard's slogan is *Veritas*, "Truth." Yale's slogan is *Lux et veritas*, "Light and Truth," and my alma mater Brandeis University's is, "Truth Even Unto its Innermost Parts." The search is not limited to only philosophers and educators. Truth detectives also include poets, novelists, artists, journalists, lawyers, and scientists.

The quest for truth affects all facets of life, even love. When we pursue truth, we find love; when we pursue love, we don't always find the truth. Perhaps it's because when one looks for love, one looks outside himself. However, when one looks for truth, one looks inside himself. Truth must precede love, hence the expression "true love."

Furthermore, Descartes believed that anyone who is thinking is searching, and the search is the act of being alive. He believed that thinking had value because it meant you were real. He made the invisible process of thought visible. The next hurdle in creating real value for ideation was jumped by an Italian.

THE GREATEST THINKER OF ALL TIME WAS PAID UP FRONT

The best example I know of a thinker being truly rewarded dates to fifteenth-century Italy. Back then the word *commission* had a very different meaning from today. Artists received a commission to create. One such thinker was Leonardo da Vinci. If you wanted to commission this extraordinary thinker, you would pay handsomely and that stipend would unleash his imagination.

At forty-three, Leonardo da Vinci would create *The Last Supper*. But first he would tell his sponsor, "Show me the money!" An interesting side note about this sponsor was his request for Leonardo to speed up. Leonardo said he liked to paint slowly. He still had not drawn Judas, and he told the sponsor that if he would sit as Judas, the work could be completed ahead of schedule. That stopped the sponsor's complaining. When the work was completed, it was a feast for the senses.

In his spare time, Leonardo studied the flight of birds. Not surprisingly, this investigative process lead him to theorize that man could fly by flapping man-made wings. It was only through incubation, however, that he reached the illumination that flying was about gliding, not just flapping wings. Five hundred years later, his illustration of flying machines sold at an auction for $30 million.

At age fifty, Leonardo again received a commission from a man who desired a simple portrait

---

THE DIVINE IDEA

MOSES WAS THE MOST INFLUENTIAL JEW BEFORE JESUS CHRIST. HIS IMPACT ON THE ANCIENT WORLD WOULD FOREVER MODERNIZE THOUGHT. THE GREEKS CONSIDER HIM TO BE ONE OF THE PILLARS OF THEIR CIVILIZATION. JOSEPHUS SAID HE INVENTED THE WORLD LAW. EUPOLEMUS SAID MOSES WAS THE FIRST WISE MAN. NUMENIUS OF APAMEA SAID THAT PLATO COPIED HIM. MOSES SAID HIS IDEAS WERE INSPIRED FROM ANOTHER SOURCE, TOO — GOD.

of his wife. Once he was paid and his monetary worries were behind him, Leonardo drew on his own soul to capture the spirit of another. Considered a minor work at the time, Leonardo's creation of the Mona Lisa became the most celebrated painting in history. Leonardo received commissions until the day he died.

Many musicians and artists are still compensated like this. However, in the art of business, most companies and people earn their commissions or fees on the back end — a fitting expression. This system prevents thinkers from drawing on the mind's magic. Money held out as a carrot is not healthy food for thought. Many people feel that if they take chances, chances are they will be fired. So they don't rock the boat. Worse yet is that when you create something for nothing, people will often treat you like nothing.

It is ironic that during the most fertile idea era of all — the Renaissance — a mathematically minded Venetian monk named Luca Pacioli — now famous among accountants — created the double-entry bookkeeping system. The concept was to fit ideas into a physical column. Ideas, of course are mental. So they ended up in what we now call "good will" or "intangibles." The truth is, the real value is in the intangible assets, not the tangible ones. The time has come for companies to audit their intangibles. They are sure to find hidden values and strengths.

Ideas are more valuable than factories, natural resources, or money itself. After all, **money doesn't create ideas, ideas create money.**

Think of your physical plant — your building, desks, and everything you manufacture — as the hardware. Now think of your employees' ideas as the software. I am reminded that IBM based its business on hardware, and Microsoft almost stole it away by making software. Are you IBM or Microsoft?

Like Leonardo da Vinci, Microsoft knows that the pictures of the mind are more valuable than the paints on the palette. Our next challenge will be to compensate thinkers like renaissance painters, instead of house painters.

THE FATHER OF OUR COUNTRY MADE ONLY A DOLLAR

Albert Einstein was correct when he said, "Imagination is more important than knowledge." More valuable, too. His theory of relativity was but a theory. No one ever traveled at the speed of light. Yet it is an idea that changed the world. Was Einstein properly compensated? No.

Imagine if Martin Luther King, Jr., and Gandhi had been financed to spread their ideas on nonviolence. Perhaps schools could have been funded years ago, before these men died, to study and proliferate tolerance and understanding.

The charismatic Shawnee chief Tecumseh united tribes in a single Native American federation, yet like his brothers, his remuneration was relocation. He received no support for his people's ideas about farming a rugged America, growing loving families, and creating respect for our precious environment.

How about Susan B. Anthony? The daughter of a Quaker abolitionist, she was fined $100 after she dared to vote in 1872. The women's rights movement needs to write her a check.

Cesar Chavez unionized farm workers, held public fasts, and helped thousands of workers attain meaningful wages and lives. While he never missed his eight children's birthdays, the paydays he missed were plenty.

What is the true value of Helen Keller's insight? And Mother Teresa's prayers? How do we pay for the justice FDR brought to the world or the inspiration JFK gave us? Abraham Lincoln's ideas touched on morality, ethics, inspiration, courage, and tenacity. Public servant or not, he brought us through the most divisive war our country will probably ever see. The closest he came to real money was having his image on pennies and the five-dollar bill. It could be worse; George Washington's face made only a dollar.

Christopher Columbus discovered America but died broke. Van Gogh rarely sold his work for more than the cost of a nightly room. Dr. Jonas Salk , the man who gave us the polio vaccine, was given a small stipend in comparison to the value of the shot he provided to children all over the world.

These might be exceptional examples. However, these people, like many of us, spent their lives thinking of ways to improve the world. And like a lot of us, their ideas were implemented though no monetary value was assigned. True, these people's legacies are worth more to us than all the money in the world. But if these great minds, who provided great ideas, had been given great amounts of money, how much richer would our lives be today? The power of a great idea is infinite. The royalties should match.

Most recently, Dolly, the cloned sheep, made headlines. Immediately, drug companies reassessed what she could do for their bottom lines, yet the researchers will probably realize only a fraction of the profit.

The argument could be made that discoverers, artists, and scientists pursue knowledge for the sheer thrill of it, but I contend that today's explorers of ideas are offering their mind's best efforts, yielding all the profit for people who are not the prophets. This, too, will change as we learn to spread the profits to the prophets.

The future will see brain power closing the largest divide known to man and woman — the space between the amount of our brain we use and its unlimited capacity. As of the writing of this work, no definition of human limit appears anywhere.

Advertising has always been somewhat of a reflection of our society. So it came as no surprise to me that on New Year's Day 1998, Nike, the world's largest shoe manufacturer, introduced its new slogan: "I Can."

"At a time when cynicism in sports is at an all-time high, 'I Can' is an effort to return to a focus on the positive," says Bob Wood, Nike Vice President of U.S.A. Marketing. "It reflects the deep emotional connection that people have with sports in feeling good about participating and setting personal goals."

I see something else going on here. In 1988,

the "Just Do It" slogan was created when an ad executive speaking to Nike employees told them, "Nike guys, you just do it." "Just Do It" not only became the single best-known ad tagline of the last decade, but also a call to action for all Americans to get off their butts and make it happen.

"Just Do It" isn't doing it anymore. People need an "I can" attitude to get to the top of the mountain. In the eighties it was the altitude one could reach in their sneakers. In the nineties it's the attitude reachable only through the mind.

IF YOU LOVE YOUR JOB, LEAVE IT

Economist Adam Smith illustrates the old way of doing things through the image of a pin factory. It's a place with specific jobs all set up in military order, all measured and rewarded for profits. If you worked hard, you were rewarded. If your profit to the company was soft, you were chucked out. I've been told the story of a man who was both an author and intellectual capital expert. He stated that a manager's work was defined in the acronym POEM: Plan, Organize, Execute, Measure. The measure of a man or woman to this day has been financial measurement. One company in the top fifty of the Fortune 500 was so single-minded in pursuit of a 20 percent return on equity that all its top executives were given underwear boldly imprinted "ROE 20%."

Tomorrow it will be a different story. Like the student who is now rewarded for his thinking instead of the answer, ideators — the people who think — will be rewarded for their ideas. Specialists will be more special than ever. Most people will be smarter than their bosses. Franklin Delano Roosevelt was this model's predecessor when he set up his Brain Trust, a group of people with specialized minds that could be harnessed to pull the weight of our nation's problems and deliver solutions to the President. Experts will replace Adam Smith's pin-makers, and as Thomas Stewart points out in his book *Intellectual Capital*, "Shareholder value is being replaced with values. Many jobs still and always will require big, expensive machines bought by someone else. But in the age of intellectual capital, the most valuable parts of those jobs have become the most essentially human tasks . . . sensing, judging, creating, and building relationships." During Adam Smith's day, the

---

THE MOST IDEAS

THOMAS ALVA EDISON INVENTED THE FOLLOWING: WAX PAPER, THE MIMEOGRAPH MACHINE, THE CARBON TELEPHONE TRANSMITTER, THE PHONOGRAPH, THE ELECTRIC LIGHT, THE MAGNETIC ORE SEPARATOR, THE RADIO VACUUM TUBE, THE MOTION-PICTURE CAMERA, THE DICTATING MACHINE, A VARIETY OF PORTLAND CEMENT, AN ELECTRIC VOTE RECORDER, THE DUPLEX AND AUTOMATIC TELEGRAPH MACHINE, A NEW KIND OF STORAGE BATTERY, AN ORE-CRUSHING MACHINE, THE PHONOGRAPH RECORD, THE CHEMICAL PHENOL, AN ELECTRIC PEN, THE THREE-WIRE ELECTRICAL WIRING SYSTEM, UNDERGROUND ELECTRIC MAINS, AN ELECTRIC RAILWAY CAR, A VERSION OF THE STOCK TICKER, AN ELECTRIC RAILROAD SIGNAL, THE LIGHT SOCKET AND LIGHT SWITCH, A METHOD FOR MAKING SYNTHETIC RUBBER FROM GOLDENROD PLANTS, AND A MACHINE THAT, IN HIS WORDS, WAS "SO SENSITIVE THAT IF THERE IS LIFE AFTER DEATH, IT WILL PICK UP THE EVIDENCE."

tools of the trade could be found at the office or factory. Today, you carry these tools between your ears.

So why work in a conventional linear atmosphere? The other day I was getting the little hair I have left on my head cut by my hairdresser Gina. Her creativity rivals most because she thinks about your hair, tries new styles, is very confident about her suggestions, and her results are always beyond your expectation.

Gina asked me about my latest book and I told her I was just finishing *Thinking for a Living.* "What's it about?" she asked. I told her the book would allow people like herself who had thinking expertise to leave their job and think for a living. The hairdresser who knew what to do with a ribbon escaped, and so could she.

We all can leave the conventional confines of our offices if we love our work. The caveat, however, is that you must be prepared for strenuous thinking. A true love of thought is a necessity — not only valuable thought, but giving our thought value.

WHAT WOULD YOU PAY FOR TOMORROW'S NEWSPAPER?

Globalization and technology are creating a demand for bigger ideas faster than ever before. This, in turn, is causing corporate nervous breakdowns — that is, companies torn between fulfilling a vision and just surviving in business.

Day-to-day tactical matters, ranging from departments merging to employees splurging, have clouded the long-term vision of many business leaders. These executives at the helms of their corporate ships can't stay the course unless they know what the course is. As a great poet once wrote, "To steer is heaven, to drift is hell." Enter the next big idea.

A meaningful idea today means success tomorrow. What would tomorrow's newspaper be worth to you today? The answer is close to what big thinking should be worth.

This corporate nervousness has created a marketplace in waiting – waiting to pay large sums for big ideas — because ideas put markets in motion. If an idea is exceptional, its velocity will have what engineers call "energy of activation," that is, the energy required to initiate a reaction or process, or in the business world, to escape the mundane.

Never before has the world been more willing to pay for thinking. Ideas have become the difference between winners and losers. As the world heralds the awesome power of ideas, we, individually, must be able to ascribe monetary value to our ideas. We need to change our thinking on how to price an idea by dispelling the notion that an idea's value is determined by what the market will bear. The more profitable thought is that **an idea's value is determined by what bearing it brings to the marketplace.** To understand this shift, we need to climb a pyramid.

THE THINKING PYRAMID

If you recall from chapter 4, Csikszentmihalyi's Triangle was constructed out of three angles —

Domain, Individual Talent, and Judges. In the center is where Creativity happens.

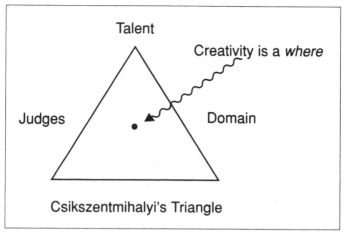

– ILLUSTRATION 1 –

The model is brilliant in that it tells us where creativity is. However, it relies on the market-place to define what the monetary value of that creativity is.

It is true that in order to be labeled creative, we must have a talent and be proficient in a domain. Furthermore, outside judges play an integral role in determining that label.

However, these critics should not determine the monetary worth of the idea. Who is to say that my idea is worth one dollar or one million dollars? Up until now, the answer would rest with the person buying. I suggest that the answer should be held by the person selling.

This, of course, is a profound shift in the valuation of ideas. How will a whole society based on business (the United States is the only country founded on the almighty dollar) change its thinking about the worth of ideas?

The answer came to me in discussions with famed author and psychologist Dr. Arthur Cohen. Together we took Csikszentmihalyi's two-dimensional triangle and created a three-dimensional triangle, which includes the outside judges, the domain, and the talent but places our Self-evaluation (or inside judge) at the very top of the triangle. The result is one of civilization's oldest ideas — the pyramid.

Like Csikszentmihalyi's triangle, one side of the pyramid represents *Domain*. The second side is *Talent*, and on the third is *Judges*. However, on top is the *All-Seeing Eye*.

By taking the triangle and making it pyramidial, we literally end up at its peak. One could say this is where potential peak profit is realized because the power is held at the top by you.

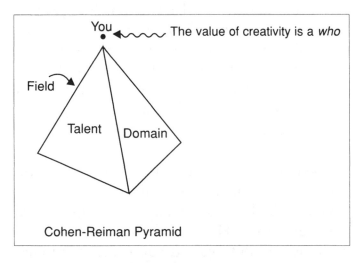

You ⟵〜〜 The value of creativity is a *who*

Field

Talent   Domain

Cohen-Reiman Pyramid

– ILLUSTRATION 2 –

Look on the back of a dollar bill for an illustration of what I'm talking about. The great seal of the United States is a pyramid with an eye on top. This illustration symbolizes the four points on the compass and the eye of God seeing above all our states. But it also serves us well as a symbol of the creative process.

Like Descartes, whose motto was "I think, therefore I am," the pyramid implies that if I think this way, then everything comes through me. This is a fresh way to think about our thinking. The process leads you to see more because you are the eye.

In order to convert from outside judgment to inside judgment, one must permit one's own ideas to function differently. This is the pivotal point of change — to focus differently on your ideas, to actually think differently; that is, to ask yourself, "Of what value is my idea?" And to answer, "Of enormous value!"

When you're situated down on the pyramid, you can see only one view, but from atop — the place all points come together — you can see it all. You, in effect, become the power-point. It is from this summit that you determine the value of your own thinking, and that thought in turn dominates Domain, Talent, and the Outside Critics or Judges.

As a metaphor, this kind of thinking gives value to our thought. It's all about loving the way you think . . . so much that you can attach real value to it. How much? As much as your ideas are worth to you. If you value your thinking, this is your most valuable asset. Outside Judges may call your ideas "fool's gold," but your imagination is worth a fortune.

This process of thinking will allow you to dictate your value in the marketplace instead of the marketplace dictating your value. If the Csikszentmihalyi Triangle locates the where of creativity, the *Cohen-Reiman Pyramid* identifies the who that's you.

SELF-WORTH DETERMINES NET WORTH

Throughout this book, I emphasize that great thinking occurs in a myriad of ways. However, the one characteristic that separates the thinker from the tinkerer is self-esteem. Economists agree. In early 1998, Gene Koretz of *Business Week* magazine wrote an article on economists Arthur H. Goldsmith of Washington and Lee University, Jonathan R. Veum of the Bureau of Labor Statistics, and William A. Darity, Jr., of the University of North Carolina, all of whom have identified a new resource for people to create wealth: psychological capital.

"Everyone knows that psychological variables, such as attitudes and personalities, can affect productivity. Yet, economists have generally shied away from studying their impact upon wages solely on the grounds that they are difficult to measure," says Goldsmith.

After conducting a national survey, the economists found that self-esteem correlated with higher wages and that higher wages increased self-esteem. "A ten percent rise in self-esteem boosted wages more than a ten percent increase in education or work experience."

The bottom line is that **your net worth is impacted by your self-worth.** This suggests that your sense of self emanates from the top of the pyramid. Your earning power begins at this peak from your own sense of self-worth and self-knowledge. As Dr. Cohen says, "The top of the pyramid is the point of departure to act in my own, enlightened self-interest as a human being."

Another implication is that the pyramid approach must start during childhood because that is the time the pillars of self-esteem are put into place. Parents and teachers need to add self-worth to the basic skills and values that children need to acquire.

To enlighten yourself is a lifelong quest that produces a sense of wholeness and self-worth. But it does more than just impart knowledge. It also sends out a clear message: My thinking is valuable. This thought is literally money in the bank. Napoleon Hill, author of *The Laws of Success*, has a favorite poem, which reads:

If you think you are beaten, you are;
If you think you dare not, you don't;
If you like to win, but you think you can't,
If is almost certain that you won't.

IDEA NET

TIM BERNERS-LEE WAS TRAINED IN PHYSICS AT OXFORD UNIVERSITY AND WAS WORKING AT THE SWISS-BASED EUROPEAN PARTICLE PHYSICS LABORATORY WHEN HE HAD A BIG *Aha!* HIS IDEA WAS TO CREATE A GLOBAL HYPERMEDIA SYSTEM FOR RESEARCHERS TO COLLABORATE ON LARGE PROBLEMS. HE NAMED THIS BABY THE "WORLD WIDE WEB." HOW MUCH PROFIT DID BERNERS-LEE MAKE ON HIS IDEA? "FOR SOMETHING LIKE THE WEB TO EXIST, IT HAS TO BE BASED ON PUBLIC, NONPROPRIETARY NEED," HE SAYS. ADVERTISERS, OF COURSE, DISAGREE.

If you think you'll lose you've lost,
For out of the world we find
Success begins with a fellow's will —
It's all in the state of mind.

If you think you are outclassed, you are —
You've got to think high to rise.
You've go to be sure of yourself before
You can ever win a prize.

Life's battles don't always go
To the stronger or faster man;
But soon or late the man who wins
Is the man who thinks he can.

Do you think enough of what you're thinking to charge for it? Perhaps the following story will help you gain perspective.

THE GREENLEES EFFECT

Over the past twenty years, I've won more than my share of creative awards. I've been called "guru," "wiz," and "genius" as well as a few pejorative terms I'd rather not print. But regardless of the accolade, I've never attached real value to those terms. Sure, my advertising agency would more often than not get the business we were pitching, but we never charged the real value of our ideas. We were not alone. That began to change, however, after a meeting I had with Michael Greenlees, the chief executive officer of GGT Worldwide, at the time the twelfth largest advertising agency in the world. Greenlees was the English gentleman who orig-inally bought Babbit & Reiman from Joel Babbit and me in June of 1988 for $5 million.

Michael had seen my agency make money and lose money. He stuck with us during some poor and hard transitional years as the agency matured. Regardless of the yearly net income, he always acknowledged my company for the barrage of bright ideas we could create. His chief financial officer, Mark Bayliss, was trained by the Murdoch organization, which had a reputation for "slash-and-burn" management. That means take no prisoners. If they don't turn a profit, turn them out to pasture. Yet both men were intrigued by and actually encouraged my love of ideas versus ads.

The turning point came while BrightHouse was still in the incubation stage in my mind. Greenlees was in Atlanta along with Bayliss to check on his U.S. enterprises.

Greenlees sat in my office, and we cradled the BrightHouse idea like two men and a baby. We talked about the concept of idea valuation and how it would change the business. I told him that advertising as we knew it had, at most, another decade to survive, and then the marketing world would know of three entities: (1) idea houses, (2) advertising agencies that would become execution houses awaiting ideas from the idea houses, and (3) the media, by then a commodities business buying space in newspapers and magazines and time on television and radio. The age of the advertising agency as we knew it was coming to an end.

Michael Greenlees looked at me and said something that would start a revolution inside my head. He said, "The secret of creating value for your ideas is the ability to look at the buyer, who respects the value of thinking, and attach a large sum of money to that idea, without smiling."

Until then, I was making millions a year through executing. Asking for one, two, or three million to handle an advertising account in exchange for ideas, execution, account handling, research, media, golf, tennis, and dinners was acceptable. But to ask that amount for just one idea? His bet was that most people, regardless of their celebrity, would indeed smile because the idea of being paid for an idea — being paid to think — was unthinkable. Just the kind of thought I loved!

HOW MUCH IS THAT IDEA IN THE WINDOW?

Ghost Myst was the world's first perfume to celebrate a woman's inner beauty, and also the first to celebrate the value of an idea. It was to be a small celebration because our contract stipulated a payment of $8,000 which, upon execution of the fragrance and national distribution, would rise to $25,000 per month. So after one year BrightHouse was paid $308,000. The profit from that sum was $40,000. The perfume generated $30 million in retail sales. My percentage, then, was .13 percent!

Some months later my wife, Cynthia, and I were having dinner with the former president of Coty, Inc., and his wife at Le Cirque in New York. The president was telling a story about his lawyer's wife who had come up with the name for a fragrance and was given a new Mercedes for thinking up the name.

Later that week, Cynthia came up with the name for Coty's new men's fragrance. I knew it was brilliant. I called Coty and gave them the name "Raw Vanilla" for their vanilla-based men's product. (A year later it would be named winner of the 1996 Men's Mass Fragrance Award from the International Fragrance Foundation.) The Mercedes never arrived, but the idea for BrightHouse shifted into high gear, as we learned that a great idea should be accompanied by a commensurate price tag. Coty agreed.

BrightHouse officially opened on June 27, 1995. Shortly afterward, a man named George Donovan, who had just been made president of the Patten Corporation, asked me to lunch. He wanted to know how much one of my ideas would cost. Michael Greenlees's voice echoed in my head. I calculated the enormous ill will the Patten Corporation was facing as a result of some recent negative publicity and balanced that with the good will I could create. I came up with a price: $75,000. I did not smile. "Just for the idea?" asked Mr. Donovan. "Yes, sir," I replied. The check came for the lunch, and the check for $75,000 followed for the idea, part of which was to rename the company bluegreen. Patten's annual revenues before the idea were $50 million; current revenues are more than $150 million. What's more, bluegreen's stock price has increased 300 percent since that lunch. George Donovan got in on the ground floor of the revolution.

After developing the 4 I's methodology, BrightHouse's rate was pegged at $450,000 per ideation session, with some contracts exceeding $1,000,000 for thinking.

We had successfully shifted our thinking from a process of "create and wait for the rate" to a process of continuous interaction among all corners of the 3-D triangle. Our thinking had become the power-point, just as all of our thinking should be. We had come a long way since a young design student had set her fee at $35 for the Nike swoosh logo, according to *Swoosh* authors J. B. Strasser and Laurie Becklund. But I'm not sure we as a society have come nearly far enough. The fact is that thinkers over time, all too often, have not received appropriate value for their thinking.

Over the past twenty years, I have won more than five hundred creative awards in national and international competitions, including the Silver Lion at the Cannes Film Festival. In addition, I have created two successful advertising companies and the world's first ideation corporation. I also named and cofounded the largest

---

AN IDEA OF HOPE

SHE WOULD WRITE IN 1943, "I DON'T THINK OF ALL THE MISERY BUT THE BEAUTY THAT REMAINS. MY ADVICE IS: GO OUTSIDE, TO THE FIELDS, ENJOY NATURE AND THE SUNSHINE, GO OUT AND TRY TO RECAPTURE HAPPINESS IN YOURSELF. THINK OF ALL THE BEAUTY THAT'S STILL LEFT IN AND AROUND YOU AND BE HAPPY." NAZI GERMANY KILLED MORE THAN SIX MILLION JEWS, INCLUDING ANNE FRANK, BUT THEY COULD NOT KILL HER PASSION FOR LIFE OR TAKE AWAY HER WEALTH, I.E., THE LOVE IN HER HEART. ANNE FRANK TEACHES US THE TRUE POWER OF WONDROUS THOUGHT.

independent bookstore chain in the southeast, Chapter 11 Bookstores — "prices so low you'll think we are going bankrupt," — and cofounded the Horseradish Grill — one of America's top restaurants, according to *Esquire* Magazine. My next culinary goal is to open a fish restaurant that would guarantee Atlantans fresh fish caught the night before. I will name the restaurant, appropriately FINOMINA.

During this time, I have brought all nine attributes of big thinking to bear on these creations, but one rule of thinking has been omnipresent: my unswerving belief that it all could happen because **I am creative**. I actually believe my mind is special. Not in a psychological way, for I am not a Mensa candidate nor does my IQ top the charts. But my self-worth has compounded over the years, yielding great returns — everything from gold awards to financial rewards.

I create big ideas because I believe I can, not because I am creative. At the top of the pyramid one has the power to create anything and create value for everything created. My climb began as a child, helped by my parents and teachers, and continued through the help of my mentors and my wife and children. All these people added to my psychological capital.

The bottom line is this: **A healthy self-worth creates a wealthy net worth.**

IT'S THE THOUGHT THAT COUNTS

How many times have you heard that expression? Yet we have never counted up the thing that counts the most — a good thought. Perhaps that is because good thoughts cannot be bought. You might say they are priceless.

Love, compassion, and service to our fellow man and woman produce wealth beyond numbers. These are acts of the heart. Why then should acts of the head be minimized? Some value short of priceless surely could be put upon our thinking.

Artists will tell us they don't create for the money — that their love for their art demands a full heart, not a full pocket. Yet so many artists, writers, and most thinkers are not compensated for acts of their hearts or their minds.

In Ayn Rand's *Atlas Shrugged* a character muses, "The man who produces an idea in any field of rational endeavor — the man who discovers new knowledge — is the permanent benefactor of humanity."

That's an invaluable thought. And if it's the thought that counts, it's time to start counting. It's time to pay the piper. Actually, these thoughts we have create light. Consider each thought you have. Perhaps one is a candle that can rid the world of darkness. How valuable is that? And what would we pay for it? The answers are it's priceless and we would pay almost anything. Which is why the idea of the next century is ideas.

AN IDEA THAT GETS UNDER MY SKIN

THE GERMAN PHYSICIST WILHELM CONRAD ROENTGEN, WHO DISCOVERED X-RAYS IN 1895, REFUSED TO APPLY FOR ANY PATENTS. HE WON THE NOBEL PRIZE, BUT DIED BROKE.

One of the ideas I hope to bring to fruition by the year 2000 is the special project commissioned by Tel Aviv University in Israel. The challenge is to create an idea that will create world peace by disseminating the need for tolerance and understanding among peoples of difference. BrightHouse thinkers created an idea that hopefully will bring not only different factions of the world together but also the fiercest marketers. Our intent is to have messages run in all media sponsored by arch rivals who have come together for a lofty cause.

One print advertisement would feature Coca-Cola and Pepsi with one glass and two straws. The headline would read "Coca-Cola and Pepsi drink to peace." AT&T and Sprint would issue a dual calling card asking their customers to make a call for hope. For Nike and Reebok, peace would be the finish line. McDonald's and Burger King would offer a new shake — a handshake, that is. Mastercard and Visa would jointly offer a statement of hope.

These ideas show us that advertising does have a way to better itself, and that is to spend time thinking about the message rather than how it can profit from the medium. We might call it ADDvertising, because it adds.

Hopefully by the next century, many different faiths will share one belief: compassionate thinking adds to the world.

CHAPTER 10

A More Thoughtful World: Why Thinking for a Living Is about More Than Thinking for a Living Wage

*"As we think in our hearts,
so we are."*
— Proverbs 23:7

WE BEGAN WITH my nutty idea of thinking for a living, which turns out to be not so nutty after all. Let me close with this afterthought, which may be the biggest thought of all.

I have to admit when I started thinking about thinking for a living, as a career path and as an idea for this book, what I had in mind was the world of work — how you can and should leverage your ideas at work in the biggest way possible, so they make money for you, not for someone else. I've found a way to think for a living. I wanted to show others how they could do it, too.

But somewhere along the line it hit me that this really wasn't just about a job. It was about thinking for a living in the broadest, most profound sense. It was about thinking for a rich, rewarding life. And it wasn't about each of us with our own private needs and dreams and agendas. It was about all of us as a global community. If this books helps you with your ideas for work, that's great. If it helps you with ideas on how to live a smarter, more joyous life, even better. But what I most want to leave you with is this idea: The human race can't afford to live stupid anymore. It's up to us collectively to find ways to reward, nurture, and encourage creative thought. Csikszentmihalyi showed us that creativity is inseparable from domain. Individual creativity is inextricably tied to the broader social environment in which it operates. The biggest hurdle the human race faces now is finding a way to create as dynamic and nurturing an environment as possible on a global scale. The scary thing is we need to do it now more than ever before. The encouraging thing is we can do it now more than ever before.

We stand on the brink of a new century, a time of unparalleled opportunity and peril. Are we prepared for it? There are some very hopeful signs. Let me mention three of them.

First of all, most of us know on some intuitive level that the era of greed, the world symbolized by Gordon Gecko in Oliver Stone's movie *Wall Street*, is over, and to grow as a country we need a less predatory model of success. I'm not sure we know what it is yet, but both politically and economically we seem to be groping for something less Darwinian than the dog-eat-dog competitiveness of the eighties.

Second, the fall of Communism around the world is the biggest affirmation of the past century that the future belongs to those most able to harness the power of bright ideas. We had a society that valued many ideas. They had a society that embraced only one idea. Who do you think wins that kind of battle? There's a lesson here. The more we're idea driven, entrepreneurial, open to opportunity, creating ideas, reinventing ourselves, the more we grow. The more we stifle ideas, sit on our lead, repeat ourselves, depend on a single model, the more we stagnate.

Third, the rise of the Internet and global communications allow us to create change on a massive, international level to a degree never before dreamed of. During the Renaissance, the rich domain that created such a revolution in art, culture, and thought was limited to a few patrons, artists, and thinkers in different parts of Europe. Now we have the potential to create a global

---

A SUPER IDEA

LOOK UP! IN CLEVELAND, OHIO! IT'S 1939! IT'S A COMIC BOOK. IT'S SUPERMAN, INVENTED BY SUPER MEN JERRY SIEGEL AND JOE SHUSTER. AFTER TRYING TO GET THEIR CAPED CRUSADER OFF THE GROUND FOR FIVE YEARS, A LUCKY BREAK LANDED THE STRIP AT ACTION COMICS. FASTER THAN A SPEEDING BULLET, SUPERMAN BECAME AN AMERICAN ICON. IN 1948, THEY ATTEMPTED TO GET THE RIGHTS TO THEIR IDEA. THEY WERE FIRED. THE CREATORS' FINANCIAL PLIGHT, HOWEVER, WOULD BECOME A SYMBOL OF THE PROFIT NOT GOING TO THE PEOPLE WHO EARNED IT.

renaissance to a degree never before imagined. We had better do it.

The inescapable truth of the twenty-first century will be that stupidity and stagnation will exact a price we can no longer afford to pay. We can't continue to destroy the environment, to burn down the earth's forests, to destroy our fisheries, to foul the air. We can't unloose our weapons of mass destruction the way humankind has stupidly resorted to war in the past. We can't allow the kind of global calamities that could occur on a planet of five billion people, likely to double in population. Just as our potential for positive change is greater than it ever was, so is our potential to unleash plagues and disasters unlike anything the world has faced in the past.

Making the right decisions will not be easy. But if my life has taught me anything, it's that there's no limit to what the human mind can achieve. Just as I believe in God on a powerful, visceral level, I believe in the healing power of human creativity in the same way. So I have to think that our future depends on just one issue: how much we can free up our creativity, reward thought, and allow all of us to become confident, creative thinkers. Once that happens, I think our potential together is limitless. **As intellectual capital becomes of greater value to humankind than concrete capital, the world will experience dramatic changes.**

The measurement of success will be based on one's ability to create from within one's mind instead outside. Idea rich will take the place of asset rich.

Our society will become more egalitarian as intellectual capital levels the playing field. Born rich or poor, black or white, high or low IQ, ideas will become the determining factor for advancement. "Striking it rich" could happen to anyone with a rich mind.

Rich minds will come from a reformation of our education system. To accommodate the need for thinkers, educators will shift from rote learning to experiential learning, from the outcome to the process. Imagine children being taught that it's more important to question than to provide an answer.

Perhaps the greatest of all impacts of idea commerce is that we will think before we act. As the price tag on thinking rises, so too will the consequences of that thinking. This will lead people to contemplate and incubate before jumping the gun and starting wars or resorting to the kind of mindless violence that has characterized so much of human history. A world in which thinking is truly valued will make the consequences of stupidity and arrogance so plain, that it will set in motion a powerful dynamic that will discourage them.

Is this naive? I don't think so. In my heart, I have to believe that thinking smarter means thinking kinder, too, and I think that's what we'll see. Compassion is a thoughtful process, as is prayer, and, God willing, we will all do a lot more of that, too. I hope this book, in some small way, plays a role in helping to create the environment in which compassion and prayer, wisdom and kindness, humility and grace become the powerful, unstoppable big ideas for the next century. If they do, thinking for a living, in the broadest sense of thinking for a rich life, will enrich us all.

EPILOGUE

OCCUPATION: THINKER

*"The privilege of a lifetime is
to be who you are."*
— JOSEPH CAMPBELL

Recently I received my two-year-old son,
Julien's, application to preschool. In the section
on family history was the line asking for the
father's occupation. I stared at it for some time.

I could be safe and write "marketing" or feel
proud and say "writer." I thought about
ideation, too. I considered the word *thinker* and
then pictured all those academic types peering
over Juilen's application and seeing his father's
occupation read "Thinker." "Who does he think
he is? Is he related to Rodin?"

Would I lose credibility? Would the school
think less of my child? Would I hurt his chances
of succeeding?

Then I had an *Aha!* My children were going to
school to learn how to think. If my occupation
is "Thinker," my children would have already
done what so many fathers egotistically pray for
— that their children will go into their dad's
business!

I had nothing to be ashamed of. Or did I?
After all, how much do thinkers make for a living? Pennies, I thought they would think. Would
they think my wife was supporting me? Well, she
does emotionally, which is all that's important,

and if she chose to, she could make more money than I ever had.

And then I had another *Aha!*

I wrote this book for people who have the same fears about thinking for a living in the hope that they would be unshackled by our society's incapability of putting real value on ideation.

My occupation is thinker and that's who I am, employed at that. Frankly, I can't wait until I get my new passport application. I'll get a kick out of writing "Thinker" in the occupation section. After all, if I'm right, thinkers will be going places in the next century.

ACKNOWLEDGMENTS

As a man thinketh, so is he. Therefore, I want to acknowledge those who I have thought about while writing this book and others who have impacted my thinking.

My thanks go to Peter Applebome. Without him this book would not be the book you read. Peter is an excellent journalist, author, and friend who helped me distill my thoughts to hopefully produce a few drops of wisdom.

To my dear friend Michael Greenlees, I want to say thanks for the Greenlees Effect and the effect he has had personally on my career in thinking. The BrightHouse model could not have been built without the bright light of BrightHouse's thinkers.

Elizabeth O'Dowd is chief creative officer of the company. Her talents have touched, molded, or created every great idea at BrightHouse. She is the consummate creator, in that Elizabeth can create out of thin air vistas as vast as the sky and images as bright as the sun. Starting in the studio at Babbit & Reiman Advertising in 1986, Elizabeth has perfected her art to the highest of elevations. She will tell you, though, she hasn't scratched the surface. This is part of the style that has created substance.

Roger Milks is chief operating officer and global strategic planner. He's been the architect of great ideas, the top detective in the search for truth, and a futurist. How much would you pay for tomorrow's newspaper? That's what Roger is worth to BrightHouse and all who enter.

Kelsey Kemple Schmidt is managing director

of BrightHouse. Kelsey is also our spiritual director. Her faith in our economic model and her unswerving respect for the value of ideas have kept us all in check.

If BrightHouse had a chief of staff, her name would be Amy Frankel, my assistant. Amy was incredibly instrumental in creating both BrightHouse and this book. She possesses enormous energy and talent. What's more, she uses these assets every minute of every day. Amy is a great idea.

I would also like to thank Steve Dorvee, our brilliant trademark attorney from the law firm of Arnall Golden & Gregory.

I would also like to acknowledge Dr. Arthur Cohen. His incredible insights over the years have added richness and life to mine. He is both a man of letters and ideas. His thoughts have touched so many more people than he could ever imagine.

If ideas live and die by the way people nuture them, then my publisher, Chuck Perry, is the father of this one. I want to thank him for his unswerving belief in this wild idea. His patience and passion made my ideas leap from my soul to the page.

The other father I would like to thank is mine. Henri Reiman's last written note to me read, "Creativity, when not used, turns to depression." I feel good today, Dad, real good. As always I thank my mother, Phyliss, for feeding my mind with thoughts of greatness, my brother, Michael, whose way of thinking has always brought joy to my life, and my Grandma Mae who has the mind of the century. And in six years, that's how old it will be.

Finally, I would like to thank my family. My sons Alden and Julien remind me every day that I should try to be more like them. They already are geniuses because they know that love is the most valuable thought of all. Which brings me to the person I dreamed of before I met her, the person I think about every second, and the woman who will be in my thoughts forever. I love you, Cynthia.

And thank God for God.

BIBLIOGRAPHY

8 Weeks to Optimum Health
Dr. Andrew Weil
Alfred A. Knopf, New York, 1997

The 100 Greatest Entrepreneurs of the Last 25 Years
A. David Silver
John Wiley & Sons, Inc., New York, 1985

2201 Fascinating Facts
David Louis
Wings Books, New York, 1983

Aha!
Jordan Ayan
Crown Trade Paperbacks, New York, 1997

The Art of Thought
Graham Wallas
Harcourt, Brace, New York, 1926

Book of Facts
Isaac Asimov
Hastings House, New York, 1992

The Brain Book
Peter Russell
Hawthorn Books, Inc., New York, 1979

Brain Longevity
Dharma Singh Khalsa, M.D., with Cameron Smith
Warner Books, New York, 1997

College Begins At Two
Isabelle Buckley
Whiteside, Inc., New York, 1965

Creating Minds
Howard Gardner
BasicBooks, New York, 1993

The Creative Process
Brewster Chiselin, Editor
University of California Press, Berkeley, 1952

Creativity
Mihaly Csikszentmihalyi
Harper Collins, New York, 1996

The Creators
Daniel J. Boorstin
Random House, New York, 1992

Disruption
Jean-Marie Dru
John Wiley & Sons, Inc., New York, 1996

Elizabeth
Alexander Walker
Zebra Books, Kensington Publishing Corp., New York, 1990

The Farmer's Almanac Book of Everyday Advice
Judson D. Hale
Random House, New York, 1995

Healing Words
Larry Dossey, M.D.
Harper San Francisco, 1993

Intellectual Capital: The New Wealth of Organizations
Thomas A. Stewart
Currency/Doubleday, New York, 1997

Jamming
John Kao
HarperBusiness, New York, 1996

The Jewish 100
Michael Shapiro
A Citadel Press Book
Carol Publishing Group, Secaucus, NJ, 1994

Jump Start Your Brain
Doug Hall with David Wecker
Warner Books, New York, 1993

Money
Andrew Hacker
Scribner, New York, 1997

The New Organizational Wealth
Karl Erik Sveiby
Berrett-Koehler, San Francisco, 1997

Organizing Genius
Warren Bennis and Patricia Ward Biederman
Addison/Wesley Publishing Company, Reading, MA, 1997

Paradigms
Joel Arthur Barker
HarperBusiness, New York, 1992

A Path with Heart
Jack Cornfield
Bantam Books, New York, 1993

Profiles of Genius
Gene N. Landrum
Prometheus Books, New York, 1993

Psychotrends
Shervert H. Frazier, M.D.
Simon & Schuster, New York, 1994

Race
J. R. Baker
Oxford University Press, USA, 1974

Real Time
Regis McKenna
Harvard Business School Press, Boston, 1997

Rethinking the Future
Edited by Rowan Gibson
Original contributions from: Warren Bennis, Stephen Covey, Eli Goldratt, Gary Hamel, Michael Hammer, Charles Handy, Kevin Kelly, Philip Kotler, John Kotter, John Naisbitt, Michael Porter, C. K. Prahalad, Al Ries, Peter Senge, Lester Thurow, and Jack Trout
Nicholas Brealey Publishing, London, 1997

Secrets from Great Minds
John H. McMurphy, Ph.D.
Amaranth Publishing, Dallas, 1991

Spontaneous Healing
Dr. Andrew Weil
Alfred A. Knopf, New York, 1995

Swoosh
The Unathorized Story of Nike
and the Men Who Played There
J. B. Strasser and Laurie Becklund
Harper Collins Publishers, Inc., New York, 1993

The Tom Peters Seminar
Tom Peters
Vintage Books, New York, 1994

Triumph of the Human Spirit
International Paralympic Committee
Disability Today Publishing Group, Inc., Oakville, Ontario,
Canada, 1997

The Virtual Corporation
William H. Davidow and Michael S. Malone
Harper Collins, New York, 1992

*A Whack on the Side of the Head: How You Can Be More
Creative*
Roger van Oech
Warner Books, New York, 1990

What Really Matters: Searching for Wisdom in America
Tony Schwartz
Bantam Books, New York, 1995

When Mothers Work
Joan K. Peters
Addison-Wesley, Reading, MA, 1997

Words I Wish I Wrote
Robert Fulghum
Harper Collins, New York, 1997

Why Didn't I Think of That?
Allyn Freeman and Bob Golden
John Wiley & Sons, Inc., New York, 1997

MAGAZINES

The Kiss.
John Grossman. Sky Magazine.
January, 1998. pgs. 62-66.

The Riddle of the Mozart Effect.
Don Campbell. Natural Health.
January-February, 1998. pgs. 114-119.

"The Speed Trap. Jim Bennett." *UTNE Reader.*
April, 1997. pgs.41-47.

IF THIS BOOK MAKES YOU THINK,
WRITE TO ME PERSONALLY.

JOEY REIMAN
BRIGHTHOUSE
790 MARIETTA ST.
ATLANTA, GA 30318
WWW.THINKBRIGHTHOUSE.COM